The Classic Rock Quiz Book

Also by Presley Love

Rock Lyrics Quiz Book

The Classic Rock Quiz Book

From the Animals to Frank Zappa

Revised and Updated

Presley Love

Citadel Press
Kensington Publishing Corp.
www.kensingtonbooks.com

CITADEL PRESS books are published by

Kensington Publishing Corp.
850 Third Avenue
New York, NY 10022

All Kensington titles, imprints, and distributed lines are available at special quantity discounts for bulk purchases for sales promotions, premiums, fund raising, educational, or institutional use. Special book excerpts or customized printings can also be created to fit specific needs. For details, write or phone the office of the Kensington special sales manager: Kensington Publishing Corp., 850 Third Avenue, New York, NY 10022, attn: Special Sales Department, phone 1-800-221-2647.

Kensington and the K logo Reg. U.S. Pat. & TM Office
Citadel Press is a trademark of Kensington Publishing Corp.

First printing 2000

10 9 8 7 6 5 4 3 2 1

Printed in the United States of America

Library of Congress Cataloging-in-Publication Data

Love. Presley.
    The classic rock quiz book : from the Animals to Frank Zappa /
Presley Love.—Rev. and updated.
        p.   cm.
    "A Citadel Press book."
    ISBN 0-8065-2080-9 (pbk.)
    1. Rock music—Miscellanea.   I. Title.
ML3534.L69   1999
781.66—dc21   98–45825
                                                    CIP
                                                    MN

To Jim Peters and deejays everywhere who have helped make rock and roll a part of our lives!

Contents

Preface

The Classic Rock Quiz Book is for music fans who want to have some fun and challenge their rock trivia knowledge. *Rock Lyrics Quiz Book,* my 1994 Citadel publication, opened up a new avenue for music enjoyment, adding a quiz format to rock of the fifties through the nineties and gaining a following of thousands. *The Classic Rock Quiz Book* is even more fun, and it is sure to add to the following of fans and deejays who love to test their rock knowledge.

Writing this book has been a gas, a true delight, because I always wanted to include key lyrics as well as little-known facts about the artists themselves, all in one book. And my favorite part is the classic rock titles section, in which the reader is challenged to identify the song from selected memorable lyrics. In all, this book is what music was meant to be: a whole lot of fun! See if you really know your music, and have your CDs handy—you're sure to want to play them once the memories are rekindled. You'll read for hours upon hours, and when you're through, you'll probably want to go through the book again!

I hope you find *The Classic Rock Quiz Book* informative as well as entertaining. This book is indeed a testament to the power of the years in which the guitar ruled the beat and lyrics secured rock and roll's place in music history. Rock and roll reached its finest moments during the classic rock years, and if you've every thought otherwise, you'll be a true believer after experiencing *The Classic Rock Quiz Book!*

Acknowledgments

The questions contained in this book come from thousands of hours of listening to various radio stations over the past many years.

The following books helped provide supplemental material, notably concerning rock artist trivia:

Rock Names by Adam Dolgins

Rock Movers and Shakers by Dafydd Rees and Luke Crampton

Top Forty Hits by Joel Whitburn

Thanks to Barbara Bower for typing and organizing the original manuscript.

What Is Classic Rock?

In 1955, music turned a page when "Rock Around the Clock" introduced the new sounds of rock and roll to a young audience. Bill Haley and His Comets weren't the first rockers, but their number one hit did indeed epitomize all that rock and roll stood for. Chuck Berry, Little Richard, and Elvis Presley, among others, rode on the crest of rock's commercial success and helped its popularity climb to new heights, ensuring its immortality in music history.

The early rockers were responsible for the success rock and roll enjoys today. Dion and the Belmonts, the Everly Brothers, the Four Seasons, and the Beach Boys helped the genre evolve through the fifties and into the early sixties, when rock and roll brought America to the forefront of music innovation. But then a funny thing happened: Hair grew longer and four lads from across the sea redefined rock and roll. The British Invasion of 1964 initiated a new period of rock and roll, and the sixties are now remembered for the groups that gave rock a new roll: the Beatles, the Rolling Stones, the Animals, the Who, and, shortly thereafter, the Yardbirds and Cream.

Many feel that classic rock began when the guitar took over the beat, when Jimi Hendrix and Eric Clapton stole the show and turned us all into guitar junkies. But in a broader sense, classic rock extends back to where the guitar sounds first gained their strength—some would credit the Stones, others feel it goes back further still, with the likes of B. B. King. There really is no consensus on which years comprise the classic rock era, just as there is no total agreement on when rock and roll really started.

To do justice to all those who feel classic rock should be limited to the mid-sixties through late seventies, I've focused on the top one hundred groups and individuals who emerged no sooner than the early sixties and whose influence extended into the mid-sixties, the seventies, and even into the eighties. And it should come as no surprise that many are still leading the rock and roll movement into the twenty-first century!

To express our indebtedness to the original rockers who may not have qualified as part of the top one hundred, the rock lyrics and rock titles sections contain questions that reach back to the earliest classics as well as those more recent. A book of rock and roll without Jerry Lee Lewis or Ricky Nelson and their contemporaries would simply be incomplete, and whether or not you feel that Bruce Springsteen and Roy Orbison are from different generations, it's hard to deny that each has become a legend of rock and roll—Bruce is "classic," Roy is "early."

I sincerely hope you enjoy our excursion into classic rock and that the comprehensive nature of the lyrics and titles sections will help remind us all that, as much as we today owe a lot to the stars of classic rock, they in turn wouldn't have made the scene without their early rock predecessors.

Rock On!

How to Use This Book

This book is divided into four sections. The first includes one hundred of the most influential classic rock artists from the mid sixties to the early eighties, including questions to test your knowledge of the song lyrics and history of each artist.

The second part includes miscellaneous trivia on various artists.

Part three is an exciting excursion through rock and roll's most memorable lyrics, testing your knowledge on specific tidbits as mentioned in the classics from the fifties through the eighties. There are four hundred rock lyrics questions that start off easy but quickly get more challenging.

The fourth part features a hodgepodge of four hundred rock titles selections from the fifties through the eighties, each citing a memorable line and then listing three possible choices, one of which is the song containing the lyrics. Like the rock lyrics questions, they get more difficult as they progress, but with a multiple-choice format, you've got a one-in-three chance of getting them correct!

Some of you will do a lot better than others, and that's the challenge to this book—see who can score the best and be crowned the King or Queen of Classic Rock!

SCORE YOURSELF:

Here's a chart to see how well you *really* know your music!
    If you score…
    80 percent (that's 4 out of every 5 answers correct) or more: You're a genuine rocker!
    60 percent (that's 3 out of every 5 answers correct) or more:

You are a little rusty and need to put more music in your life. 40 percent or less (that's 2 or less correct per 5 answers): You need to add more classic rock and roll to your life before it's too late!

I

From Aerosmith to ZZ Top: Classic Rock Artist Questions

Aerosmith

1. What was Aerosmith's first single to break into the Top Forty?
   a. "Last Child"
   b. "Sweet Emotion"
   c. "Dream On"

2. In what movie did Aerosmith appear, portraying villains?
   a. *Jesus Christ Superstar*
   b. *Sgt. Pepper's Lonely Hearts Club Band*
   c. *Tommy*

3. Which Aerosmith song was redone as a rap hit ten years later?
   a. "Walk This Way"
   b. "Dude (Looks Like a Lady)"
   c. "Angel"

4. In "Sweet Emotion," what can't Aerosmith say?
   a. why they feel the way they do
   b. where they'll be in a year
   c. if love is really the cure

5. In "Dream On," where does Aerosmith say half their life can be found?
   a. in books
   b. in the sewers of L.A.
   c. in the words of a song

Air Supply

1. From what country did Air Supply originate?
   a. Sweden
   b. Australia

   c. England

2. Which Air Supply song was their only one to reach number one?

   a. "The One That You Love"
   b. "Lost in Love"
   c. "All Out of Love"

3. Before they found out that "Even the Nights Are Better," how did Air Supply feel?

   a. that only the days held the sunlight
   b. cold and unforgiven
   c. that they were the lonely ones

4. What does Air Supply want to do in their "Sweet Dreams"?

   a. ride the skies
   b. make sweet love to you
   c. never wake up

5. In "Here I Am," what comes crashing through for Air Supply?

   a. reality
   b. memories
   c. heartache

America

1. Many rockers likened the voice of lead singer Dewey Bunnel in "A Horse With No Name" to that of another 1972 rocker. Who was he?

   a. James Taylor
   b. Neil Young
   c. Don McLean

2. Besides "A Horse With No Name," what other America hit reached number one?

   a. "Tin Man"

   b. "You Can Do Magic"
   c. "Sister Golden Hair"

3. What advice does America give to all the "Lonely People"?
   a. you're the heart and soul of rock and roll
   b. don't give up until you drink from the silver cup
   c. you'll find one day that everyone feels the same way

4. What does America say "Tin Man" got from Oz?
   a. nothing that he didn't already have
   b. a heart
   c. an incurable tan

5. In "Ventura Highway," what do some people say to America about the town?
   a. it's a tourist trap
   b. it doesn't look good in snow
   c. you can never go home from there

Animals

1. Under what name did the Animals first record?
   a. the Wild Cats
   b. the Newcastle Knights
   c. the Alan Price Combo

2. With what group did leader Eric Burdon record after leaving the Animals?
   a. Santana
   b. War
   c. Foghat

3. What do the Animals say the "Sky Pilot" will never do?
   a. reach the sky
   b. come back down to earth
   c. become the solution for peace

4. In "It's My Life," although the Animals say they'll wear sable some day, what are they now wearing?
   a. mink
   b. rags
   c. overalls

5. In "The House of the Rising Sun," what are the Animals going back to New Orleans to do?
   a. tear the house down
   b. wear that ball and chain
   c. get a full-time job

Association

1. What was the Association's biggest hit?
   a. "Windy"
   b. "Cherish"
   c. "Never My Love"

2. Before being named the Association, what name had they considered?
   a. the Hexagrams
   b. the Troubadours
   c. the Aristocrats

3. According to the Association in "Cherish," what word more than applies to the feeling when they know they won't share in your dreams?
   a. perish
   b. bummer
   c. loneliness

4. According to the Association, what kind of eyes has "Windy" got?
   a. sexy
   b. stormy
   c. soft

5. In "Never My Love," the Association questions how you can think their love will end after they have asked you to _____.
    a. help them spend their money
    b. spend your whole life with them
    c. spend the night with them

Bachman-Turner Overdrive

1. Which country did Bachman-Turner Overdrive come from?
    a. Canada
    b. England
    c. the USA

2. What sixties group did Bachman-Turner Overdrive evolve from?
    a. the Kingsmen
    b. the Grass Roots
    c. the Guess Who

3. Because they're "Taking Care of Business," what does Bachman-Turner Overdrive like to do all day?
    a. make lots of money
    b. work at nothing
    c. make love to you

4. In "You Ain't Seen Nothin' Yet," what did the doctor tell Bachman-Turner Overdrive about love?
    a. there's no medicine that can cure it
    b. you can't live with or without it
    c. any love is good love

5. In "Let It Ride," although you can't see the morning, what does Bachman-Turner Overdrive say they can see?
    a. your eyes

   b. where you're going
   c. the light

Bad Company

1. From what did Bad Company select their name?
   a. a song from the 1890's
   b. a 1972 movie
   c. a brand of jeans

2. On what label did Bad Company record all their top U.S. hits?
   a. A&M
   b. I.R.S.
   c. Swan Song

3. From which group did members of Bad Company *not* evolve?
   a. the Guess Who
   b. King Crimson
   c. Free

4. According to Bad Company in "Bad Company," what is destiny?
   a. a rising sun
   b. the future looking back
   c. a rodeo

5. What is it that Bad Company "Can't Get Enough" of ?
   a. the truth
   b. your love
   c. peace of mind

Badfinger

1. Who wrote Badfinger's first hit, "Come and Get It"?
   a. Tommy James

    b. Paul McCartney
    c. Sonny Bono

2. Who produced Badfinger's last two hits, "Day After Day" and "Baby Blue"?
    a. Billy J. Kramer, David Bowie
    b. George Harrison, Todd Rundgren
    c. James Taylor, Eric Clapton

3. According to Badfinger, what didn't "Baby Blue" think they'd forget?
    a. the way she looked that night
    b. the things that made her blue
    c. the special love they had for her

4. What does Badfinger give "Day After Day" to you?
    a. their love
    b. promises they can't keep
    c. new hope

5. What is it that Badfinger has that you can "Come and Get It"?
    a. money
    b. love
    c. V.D.

Beach Boys

1. Which of the following was *not* a name the Beach Boys used before their surfing fame?
    a. Kenny and the Cadets
    b. the Surfers
    c. the Pendletones

2. Who recorded with the earliest Beach Boys but was then trimmed from their lineup shortly after their first album?
    a. David Marks

   b. Al Jardine
   c. Bruce Johnston

3. What was the Beach Boys' first number one hit?
   a. "I Get Around"
   b. "Surfin' U.S.A."
   c. "Help Me, Rhonda"

4. Which Beach Boys song featured cheerleading?
   a. "Be True to Your School"
   b. "When I Grow Up (to Be a Man)"
   c. "Heroes and Villains"

5. Which famous solo performer toured in 1965 as a Beach Boy when Brian Wilson quit performing?
   a. Brian Hyland
   b. Lou Christie
   c. Glen Campbell

6. Which Top Ten hit was actually an adaptation of a Chuck Berry hit?
   a. "Barbara Ann"
   b. "Surfin' U.S.A."
   c. "Sloop John B"

7. In "Surfin' Safari," the Beach Boys claim that surfing is getting more popular every day, from Hawaii to the shores of _____.
   a. Madagascar
   b. Florida
   c. Peru

8. Although the Beach Boys were going to get married in "Help Me Rhonda," what happened?
   a. they lost the wedding ring
   b. the surf came up and they had to leave
   c. she let another guy come between them

9. In "Dance, Dance, Dance," the radio does the trick when who is by the side of the Beach Boys?

    a. their chick
    b. their friend Nick
    c. their mechanic

10. In "Don't Worry Baby," the Beach Boys' girlfriend makes them come alive and makes them want to ___.
    a. drive
    b. cry
    c. hide

Beatles

1. Who was the original manager of the Beatles?
    a. George Martin
    b. Mickie Most
    c. Brian Epstein

2. At what famous British club in Liverpool did the Beatles make their debut?
    a. the Casbah Club
    b. the Star-Club
    c. the Cavern Club

3. Which of the following names did the Beatles *not* record under?
    a. the Quarrymen
    b. the Beatmakers
    c. the Silver Beatles

4. Who was the original fifth Beatle?
    a. Billy Fury
    b. Stu Sutcliffe
    c. Peter Asher

5. On what famous U.S. variety show did the Beatles break into the American music scene?
    a. *The Ed Sullivan Show*
    b. *Hullabaloo*

   c. *Dick Clark's American Bandstand*

6. What was the Beatles' first number one hit in the USA?

   a. "She Loves You"
   b. "Love Me Do"
   c. "I Want to Hold Your Hand"

7. Why was Ringo Starr missing during the mid-1964 world tour?

   a. he was afraid of flying
   b. he was stricken with tonsillitis
   c. due to a contract dispute with Decca

8. What other famous rock-idol-to-be appeared on the now-famous first *The Ed Sullivan Show* featuring the Beatles in 1964?

   a. David Cassidy (Partridge Family)
   b. Elton John
   c. David Jones

9. What have been named Lennon, McCartney, Harrison, and Starr to ensure immortality for the Beatles?

   a. four British cars
   b. the trophies given out at the New Musical Express annual awards
   c. four asteroids

10. In "I Want to Hold Your Hand," how do the Beatles say they feel when they touch you?

   a. powerful
   b. confused
   c. happy

11. In "Please Please Me," what do the Beatles say it's so hard to do?

   a. reason with you
   b. please you
   c. keep from begging for more

12. In "I Feel Fine," what does the Beatles' girlfriend tell them all the time?
     a. that she's theirs
     b. what to do
     c. how well they sing

13. According to the Beatles, what does the "Nowhere Man" have command over?
     a. the world
     b. nothing
     c. his own life

14. In "Roll Over Beethoven," what warning do the Beatles give?
     a. not to step on their shoes
     b. not to say goodbye
     c. not to fight their love

15. From what city did the Beatles fly as they returned "Back in the USSR"?
     a. Miami
     b. New York City
     c. Hamburg

16. The Beatles say that whether there's "Rain" or sunshine, it's just _____.
     a. another day
     b. a waste of time
     c. a state of mind

17. In "Revolution," what do the Beatles say when you talk about destruction?
     a. you can count them out
     b. sometimes there's no other way
     c. it's a new sensation

18. In "Get Back," where do the Beatles say JoJo's home was?
     a. Tucson

    b. Albuquerque

    c. San Diego

19. In "Come Together," the Beatles say he's got to be good lookin' because he's so —————————.

    a. popular

    b. proud and vain

    c. hard to see

20. According to the Beatles, what is "The Word"?

    a. peace

    b. the bird

    c. love

Blondie

1. Deborah Harry first sang in a late-sixties folk-rock band that was named after a book about small animals. What was the name of this group?

    a. Ben and the Rodents

    b. Willard

    c. Wind in the Willows

2. Blondie had four number one hits. Which one was number one for the longest period of time?

    a. "Call Me"

    b. "Heart of Glass"

    c. "Rapture"

3. In "The Tide Is High," what does Blondie say they want to be?

    a. on higher ground

    b. your number one

    c. stupid and free

4. In "Heart of Glass," why does Blondie say love is so confusing?

    a. it was meant to be that way

    b. there's no peace of mind

    c. lovers are always guessing

5. According to Blondie in "Rapture," what happens after the man from Mars shoots you?

    a. you bleed on his feet

    b. he eats your head

    c. he makes the pain go away

Boston

1. What prompted the band to call themselves Boston?

    a. although from Chicago, they couldn't use that name—it was already taken—so they selected another city name

    b. the members were all from Boston

    c. the Standell's song "Dirty Water," a tribute to Boston

2. From what college did Boston leader Tom Scholz graduate?

    a. Boston College

    b. MIT

    c. Julliard

3. What Boston single topped the U.S. charts for two weeks?

    a. "Amanda"

    b. "Don't Look Back"

    c. "More Than a Feeling"

4. When does Boston say there's "More Than a Feeling"?

    a. when they hear that old song being played

    b. every single day of their life

    c. when words cannot express their love

5. What doesn't Boston care about doing as long as they have their "Peace of Mind"?

a.   getting behind
b.   making love until they're blind
c.   living with their own kind

David Bowie

1. What was the name of David Bowie's original backup band?
    a.   the Lower Third
    b.   the Girls
    c.   the Mothers of Invention

2. Why didn't David Bowie sing under his birth name, David Jones?
    a.   he didn't like its initials, DJ
    b.   there was already a famous Davy Jones
    c.   a Buddhist guru suggested the new name for spiritual reasons

3. "Changes" was David Bowie's first U.S. RCA release. What was his first number one RCA hit?
    a.   "Space Oddity"
    b.   "Fame"
    c.   "Young Americans"

4. What separated David Bowie from other male performers in his 1970s concerts?
    a.   he sang in a high falsetto voice
    b.   he had no musical backup band
    c.   he often wore dresses

5. With whom did David Bowie sing a Christmas duet in 1982?
    a.   George Burns
    b.   Luciano Pavorotti
    c.   Bing Crosby

Jackson Browne

1. What was Jackson Browne's highest-charting single?
   a. "Somebody's Baby"
   b. "Doctor My Eyes"
   c. "Running on Empty"

2. Which song did Jackson Browne cowrite with Glenn Frey, later to become the Eagles first Top Twenty hit?
   a. "Take It Easy"
   b. "Witchy Woman"
   c. "Lyin' Eyes"

3. In "Doctor My Eyes," what feeling has Jackson Browne got?
   a. that you don't love him anymore
   b. that it's later than it seems
   c. that jealousy has gotten the better of him

4. In "Running on Empty," although Jackson Browne is running into the sun, what does he add?
   a. he's headed in the wrong direction
   b. he's running behind
   c. he's burning up

5. What does Jackson Browne say will happen with "Somebody's Baby"?
   a. she's going to have a heartache tonight
   b. nothing that hadn't been done a million times before
   c. he's going to make her his tonight

Buckinghams

1. What was the Buckinghams' first hit, and only number one hit?
   a. "Kind of a Drag"

    b. "Mercy, Mercy, Mercy"

    c. "Don't You Care"

2. What were they called before naming themselves the Buckinghams?

    a. the Leftovers

    b. the Pulsations

    c. the Portraits

3. The Buckinghams wonder, in "Don't You Care," why you keep on _____ if you still love them.

    a. running around with other guys

    b. putting them down

    c. hanging up when they call

4. Since knowing "Susan," what do the Buckinghams say they have been losing?

    a. their minds

    b. sleep

    c. all their other friends

5. When do the Buckingham's say it's "Kind of a Drag"?

    a. when your socks don't match

    b. when your baby doesn't love you

    c. when your parents don't let you go out

Buffalo Springfield

1. After what did the Buffalo Springfield name themselves?

    a. an Indian tribe

    b. a rifle

    c. a steamroller

2. Which of the following groups was *not* an offshoot of the Buffalo Springfield?

    a. the Flying Burrito Brothers

    b. Crosby, Stills, Nash and Young

    c. Poco

3. Which well-known rocker joined the Buffalo Springfield on stage during their 1967 appearance at the Monterey Pop Festival?

    a. David Crosby

    b. Jimi Hendrix

    c. Paul McCartney

4. In "For What It's Worth," the Buffalo Springfield deduce that nobody's right if _____.

    a. nobody's left

    b. everybody's wrong

    c. no one really cares

5. In "On the Way Home," how can you tell Buffalo Springfield's dream is real?

    a. by the look in their eyes

    b. because home is where the heart is

    c. because they love you

Byrds

1. Why did the Byrds select the unusual spelling for their name?

    a. to poke fun at the movie *Bye Bye Birdie*

    b. so as not to be confused with "birds," a British slang for "girls"

    c. to express their allegiance to Bob Dylan

2. Which of the following was *not* a name used before they were called the Byrds?

    a. the Beefeaters

    b. the Jet Set

    c. the Mugwumps

3. What was the Byrds' last single to reach the Top Forty charts?
   a. "My Back Pages"
   b. "So You Want to Be a Rock 'n' Roll Star"
   c. "Eight Miles High"

4. Which member of the original group later became part of a highly successful trio?
   a. Gene Clark
   b. David Crosby
   c. Chris Hillman

5. In "So You Want to Be a Rock 'n' Roll Star," what musical instrument do the Byrds say you should learn how to play?
   a. a complete set of drums
   b. a tambourine
   c. an electric guitar

Cheap Trick

1. Which of the following was *not* a former band name for the members of Cheap Trick?
   a. Fuse
   b. Chicken Funk
   c. Sick Man of Europe

2. In which city were all the original members of Cheap Trick born?
   a. London, England
   b. Sydney, Australia
   c. Rockford, Illinois

3. In which country did Cheap Trick's 1978 concerts sell out within two hours?
   a. England
   b. Japan
   c. Australia

4. What was Cheap Trick's only number one hit?
   a. "I Want You to Want Me"
   b. "The Flame"
   c. "Don't Be Cruel"

5. Where does Cheap Trick say the "Dream Police" are chasing them?
   a. inside their brain
   b. everywhere they go
   c. in your dreams

Chicago

1. Why did Chicago shorten their name from Chicago Transit Authority?
   a. it wouldn't fit on their album cover
   b. it sounded too much like a government agency
   c. they were threatened with a lawsuit

2. What was unique about the titles of Chicago's albums?
   a. each subsequent album title began with a different letter
   b. they were all drawn by a spray paint master
   c. each was numbered

3. Which Chicago member scored two solo number one hits in 1986?
   a. Robert Lamm
   b. Peter Cetera
   c. Terry Kath

4. In "25 or 6 to 4," what is Chicago getting up to do?
   a. rearrange their life
   b. cash in their chips
   c. splash their face

5. In "Old Days," what does Chicago say about memories?
   a. they are gone like yesterday's dreams

   b. they seem like yesterday
   c. they live on forever

Eric Clapton

1. Which of the following groups did Eric Clapton *not* form?
   a. the Yardbirds
   b. Cream
   c. Blind Faith

2. What was Eric Clapton's only number one hit in the seventies and eighties?
   a. "Lay Down Sally"
   b. "Layla"
   c. "I Shot the Sheriff"

3. In "Lay Down Sally," what does Eric Clapton say there's nothing wrong with wanting to do?
   a. having you stay there with him
   b. becoming a movie star
   c. making love to you

4. What is Eric Clapton going to play with "After Midnight"?
   a. your tambourine
   b. the lights
   c. his guitar

5. Where has "Layla" got Derek and the Dominos?
   a. in the palm of her hand
   b. in paradise
   c. on their knees

Dave Clark Five

1. Who was the lead singer of the Dave Clark Five?

   a. Mike Smith
   b. Denis Payton
   c. Dave Clark

2. Which song was the only number one hit for the Dave Clark Five?
   a. "Over and Over"
   b. "Because"
   c. "Glad All Over"

3. Since what event have the Dave Clark Five been in "Bits and Pieces"?
   a. since they first arrived in town
   b. since you left them
   c. since they met you

4. In "Can't You See That She's Mine," how long do the Dave Clark Five say they've been together with their girlfriend?
   a. a week
   b. a year
   c. a long time

5. In "Because," why do the Dave Clark Five want to be given a chance to be near you?
   a. because they love you
   b. because they want to know if you're for real
   c. because they want to know your name

Joe Cocker

1. What was the name of Joe Cocker's forty-three-piece band?
   a. the Compass Pointers
   b. Mad Dogs and Englishmen
   c. the British Connection

2. In which historic music festival did Joe Cocker appear and then reprise?

    a. Newport Folk Festival

    b. Monterey

    c. Woodstock

3. What was the reason for Joe Cocker's on-stage spastic movements?

    a. an uncontrollable reaction to stage fright

    b. Ray Charles's piano-playing style

    c. an early childhood condition

4. In "Feeling Alright," how does Joe Cocker say he's feeling?

    a. pretty fine

    b. he can't really say

    c. not too good

5. In "Up Where We Belong," what do Joe Cocker and Jennifer Warnes say that some people hang on to?

    a. dreams that will never come true

    b. one another in time of need

    c. what used to be

Cream

1. Why did Eric Clapton, Jack Bruce, and Ginger Baker call themselves Cream?

    a. they wanted a household word that people used daily

    b. it was a shortened form of an original name, Crushed Dream

    c. because they considered themselves the "cream of the crop"

2. George Harrison performed a guitar lick on "Badge." On what Beatles song did Eric Clapton play lead guitar?

    a. "While My Guitar Gently Weeps"

    b. "Nowhere Man"

    c. "Here Comes the Sun"

3. In "Strange Brew," what does Cream wonder?
   a. What's cooking?
   b. What's inside of you?
   c. Who are you?

4. According to Cream in "Sunshine of Your Love," the darkness approaches as lights close _____.
   a. the day
   b. the tired eyes
   c. and love grows

5. What color were the curtains in Cream's "White Room"?
   a. black
   b. ivory
   c. red

Creedence Clearwater Revival

1. Before reaching fame as C.C.R., what were they known as?
   a. Fantasy
   b. the Golliwogs
   c. Willy and the Poor Boys

2. After what famous beer is Creedence Clearwater Revival named?
   a. Olympia
   b. Hamms
   c. Coors

3. What natural disaster do Creedence Clearwater Revival fear in "Bad Moon Rising"?
   a. a hurricane
   b. an earthquake
   c. a volcano exploding

4. How long ago did Creedence Clearwater Revival head out on the road to "Lodi"?

   a. a year

   b. a month

   c. an hour

5. While "Lookin' Out My Back Door," what do Creedence Clearwater Revival see the statues wearing?

   a. high heels

   b. flower leis

   c. smiles

Crosby, Stills and Nash (and Young)

1. From what three sixties bands did Crosby, Stills, Nash and Young evolve?

   a. Jefferson Airplane/Yardbirds/Zombies

   b. Canned Heat/Spirit/Grass Roots

   c. Byrds/Buffalo Springfield/Hollies

2. According to Crosby, Stills, Nash and Young, how many died in "Ohio"?

   a. more than words can say

   b. twelve

   c. four

3. In "Teach Your Children," what do Crosby, Stills, Nash and Young say you should feed your children with?

   a. words of kindness

   b. your dreams

   c. a spoonful of love

4. Because so much time has been "Wasted on the Way," what do Crosby, Stills and Nash want to have carry them away?

   a. the water

   b. your love

   c. all the memories and the tears

5. In "Woodstock," what did Crosby, Stills, Nash and Young dream happened to the bomber jet planes riding shotgun in the sky?

   a. they turned into butterflies
   b. they were shot down
   c. they headed for Viet Nam

Deep Purple

1. From what did Deep Purple derive their name?
   a. a Boris Karloff thriller
   b. a 1963 hit song
   c. their favorite color

2. Which American group did the British Deep Purple emulate?
   a. Tommy James and the Shondells
   b. the Jimi Hendrix Experience
   c. Vanilla Fudge

3. Which flaming concert provided the spark for Deep Purple's 1973 hit "Smoke on the Water"?
   a. the Who at the Monterey Pop Festival
   b. Frank Zappa and the Mothers at Montreaux
   c. the Rolling Stones at Altamount

4. In "Hush," what does Deep Purple say they thought they heard their girlfriend doing?
   a. telling lies behind their back
   b. talking in her sleep
   c. calling their name

5. What does "My Woman From Tokyo" make Deep Purple feel like?
   a. a king
   b. a star
   c. a river

Dire Straits

1. Which of the following was *not* an occupation of vocalist Mark Knopfler before he formed Dire Straits?

a. journalist
b. social worker
c. part-time teacher

2. Which famous British rocker added vocals—and his own melody—into Dire Straits' biggest hit, "Money for Nothing"?
   a. Sting
   b. Elton John
   c. Billy Idol

3. Which rock group did Dire Straits tour with during their first UK gig?
   a. the Rolling Stones
   b. the Clash
   c. Talking Heads

4. According to Dire Straits in "Walk of Life," what is Johnny doing?
   a. traveling across the USA
   b. singing the oldies
   c. smoking cigarettes

5. According to Dire Straits in "Sultans of Swing," why doesn't Harry mind if he makes the scene or not?
   a. he's got a girl waiting for him at home
   b. he's not a fan of the music
   c. he's got a daytime job

Doobie Brothers

1. With what is the name Doobie Brothers associated?
   a. a joint
   b. the bee on *Romper Room*
   c. the cartoon character Scooby Doo

2. "Black Water" was the Doobie Brothers' first number one hit. What was their second and final number one release?

    a. "What a Fool Believes"
    b. "Takin' It to the Streets"
    c. "Real Love"

3. In "Listen to the Music," what do the Doobie Brothers say the people need?
    a. a stereo and a set of headphones
    b. a hand to hold and a love to share
    c. a way to make them smile

4. According to the Doobie Brothers, around what major city is "China Grove" located?
    a. Peking
    b. San Antonio
    c. New Orleans

5. In "Takin' It to the Streets," who do the Doobie Brothes say they are?
    a. your brother
    b. your lover
    c. your dealer

Doors

1. From what book did the Doors get their group's name?
    a. *The Doors of Perception*
    b. *Unlocking the Doors of the Imagination*
    c. *Through the Doors of Time*

2. What line were the Doors asked to alter or omit when they performed "Light My Fire" on *The Ed Sullivan Show* in 1967?
    a. "girl, we couldn't get much higher"
    b. "try to set the night on fire"
    c. "come on baby, light my fire"

3. What did Jim Morrison allegedly do during a concert in Miami, Florida, that later got him arrested?

   a. he set the drums on fire
   b. he hosted a pot party between sets
   c. he exposed himself on stage

4. According to the Doors in "Riders on the Storm," who is waiting on the road?
   a. a killer
   b. your neighbor
   c. a lover

5. In "People Are Strange," the Doors say that people are wicked _____.
   a. when you're unwanted
   b. when you've just come to a new school
   c. when you look to others for support

Bob Dylan

1. What was Bob Dylan's birth name?
   a. Robert Weberman
   b. Robert Zimmerman
   c. Robert Weisberg

2. Which of the following people did Dylan consider a major influence in his early career?
   a. Woody Guthrie
   b. Pete Seeger
   c. Dylan Thomas

3. What event in Bob Dylan's life changed his musical style, leading to a more introspective and simpler, often religious focus?
   a. a motorcycle accident
   b. a bitter divorce
   c. the death of his mother

4. According to Bob Dylan in "The Times They Are A-Changin'," what will happen if the people don't start swimming?

    a. they'll sink like a stone
    b. they'll fall further behind
    c. the world will fall in ruins

5. What does Bob Dylan hope will happen to the "Masters of War"?
    a. they'll make the world a better place
    b. they'll get their act together
    c. they'll die soon

Eagles

1. Which sixties American group had a lasting influence on the Eagles, including their name selection as well as their musical style?
    a. the Turtles
    b. the Byrds
    c. Jefferson Airplane

2. Which of the following groups did *not* contribute any members to the Eagles?
    a. Poco
    b. the Flying Burrito Brothers
    c. America

3. Which Eagles song won the Grammy award for 1977 Record of the Year?
    a. "Hotel California"
    b. "New Kid in Town"
    c. "Life in the Fast Lane"

4. In "Hotel California," what did the Eagles hear that made them think this might be heaven or hell?
    a. your voice
    b. and old Chuck Berry tune
    c. a mission bell

5. In "Peaceful, Easy Feeling," what did the Eagles find out a long time ago?

a. that love doesn't always call you by name
b. what a woman can do to your soul
c. that nights are forever without you

Electric Light Orchestra

1. What Electric Light Orchestra song was a remake of a minor hit by their earlier incarnation, the Move?
   a. "Telephone Line"
   b. "Don't Bring Me Down"
   c. "Do Ya"

2. From which 1980 film did Electric Light Orchestra score three Top Twenty hits, including the title track?
   a. *The Gambler*
   b. *Grease*
   c. *Xanadu*

3. In "Livin' Thing," what does Electric Light Orchestra say is like magic?
   a. sailing away on the crest of a wave
   b. waking up to see the break of day
   c. watching you turn and walk slowly away

4. What does Electric Light Orchestra tell the "Evil Woman" that she'd better do?
   a. get on board the very next train
   b. put her spell on some other fool
   c. change her evil ways

5. According to Electric Light Orchestra, who's got a "Strange Magic"?
   a. the blackjack dealers in Vegas
   b. they do
   c. you do

Emerson, Lake and Palmer

1. What group did singer Greg Lake leave just prior to forming Emerson, Lake and Palmer?
   a. the Small Faces
   b. the Nice
   c. King Crimson

2. What supergroup did Carl Palmer help form soon after leaving ELP?
   a. Styx
   b. Asia
   c. Supertramp

3. Although "Still...You Turn Me On," what do Emerson, Lake and Palmer say about their love for you?
   a. it doesn't make sense
   b. it's getting stronger by the day
   c. it was meant to be

4. While talking about the "Tiger in a Spotlight," what do Emerson, Lake and Palmer ask?
   a. Is their love tough enough for you?
   b. Have you ever wondered why?
   c. Can they be your tiger for a night?

5. According to Emerson, Lake and Palmer, what was the "Lucky Man" carried atop?
   a. a lucky star
   b. a gold-covered mattress
   c. a silver-lined cloud of other people's dreams

Fleetwood Mac

1. With what famous blues band did three of the original members of Fleetwood Mac play?
   a. the Blues Project

b. the Blues Magoos

c. John Mayall's Bluesbreakers

2. What was the group's only number one U.S. hit?

   a. "Dreams"

   b. "Go Your Own Way"

   c. "Hold Me"

3. What Fleetwood Mac song became the presidential theme song for Bill Clinton's successful 1992 campaign?

   a. "Little Lies"

   b. "Don't Stop"

   c. "You Make Loving Fun"

4. According to Fleetwood Mac in "Sara," what would everyone love to do in the sea of love?

   a. make love to her

   b. ride on top of the waves

   c. drown

5. In "Don't Stop," what does Fleetwood Mac say will happen if you open your eyes and look at the day?

   a. you'll see things in a different way

   b. you'll miss what the nighttime passes your way

   c. you'll find that it soon slips away

Foreigner

1. Why was Foreigner a suitable name for the group?

   a. they liked to tour overseas

   b. because of their new music style

   c. because the members were from both the U.S. and England

2. What famous sixties musician played saxophone in Foreigner's "Urgent"?

   a. Gary U.S. Bonds

   b. Junior Walker

   c. Stan Getz

3. "I Want to Know What Love Is" spent two weeks in the number one position. What song spent ten weeks in the number two position three years earlier?

   a. "Hot Blooded"
   b. "Double Vision"
   c. "Waiting for a Girl Like You"

4. According to Foreigner in "I Want to Know What Love Is," what has there been too much of in their life?

   a. promises and more promises
   b. wishing and hoping
   c. heartache and pain

5. What does Foreigner say is "Cold As Ice"?

   a. your love for them
   b. your stare
   c. their feeling for you

Peter Frampton

1. What two British bands was English-born Peter Frampton in during the late sixties?

   a. the Herd and Humble Pie
   b. the Fourmost and Blind Faith
   c. the Shindogs and Spooky Tooth

2. Before shortening his group name to Frampton, what was the band called?

   a. Peter and the Frampton Four
   b. Frampton's Camel
   c. Pframpton Pfrog

3. Which double-album set, released in 1976, went on to sell over 10 million copies worldwide?

   a. *Frampton Comes Alive*
   b. *Somethin's Happening*

   c. *I'm in You*

4. In "Show Me the Way," what is the only thing Peter Frampton can relate to?

   a. the sea
   b. heartaches
   c. the lonely stars in the sky

5. In "Baby, I Love Your Way," why does Peter Frampton ask you not to hesitate?

   a. the evening's getting late
   b. they're being guided by the hand of fate
   c. your love won't wait

Genesis

1. Which sixties British singer, now top record producer, named the group Genesis?

   a. Jonathan King
   b. Peter Asher
   c. Leapy Lee

2. Who was the original lead singer of Genesis?

   a. Denny Laine
   b. Peter Gabriel
   c. Eric Clapton

3. How did Phil Collins join Genesis as drummer in 1970?

   a. he met them at a party
   b. he responded to a music magazine ad
   c. he dated the guitarist's sister

4. What mid-eighties group did original Genesis guitarist Mike Rutherford form?

   a. Survivor
   b. Wham!
   c. Mike + the Mechanics

5. What does Genesis say happens when the girl with the "Invisible Touch" crawls under your skin?

    a. you've got an urge to scratch
    b. love will soon bite
    c. you're never quite the same

Grand Funk (Railroad)

1. What Canadian transportation company inspired the group name, Grand Funk Railroad?
   a. the Grand Trunk Railroad
   b. the Grand Junk Railroad
   c. the Graham Funk Trail-load

2. Who produced Grand Funk's first number one hit, "We're an American Band"?
   a. Bruce Springsteen
   b. Todd Rundgren
   c. Alice Cooper

3. What number one song in the sixties did the band cover and take to the top of the charts in the seventies?
   a. "Some Kind of Wonderful"
   b. "The Loco-Motion"
   c. "Walk Like a Man"

4. In "Closer to Home," what does Grand Funk Railroad want you to do?
   a. steer them in the right direction
   b. go far away from them
   c. return them their ship

5. What do you need to do "The Loco-Motion"?
   a. a little bit of rhythm and a lot of soul
   b. a party atmosphere and a whole lot of beer
   c. a few friends and a whole lot of nerve

Grass Roots

1. What was the Grass Roots' highest-charting single?

   a. "Sooner or Later"
   b. "Midnight Confessions"
   c. "Let's Live for Today"

2. What do the Grass Roots say "Two Divided by Love" can only be?
   a. sad
   b. incomplete
   c. tragic

3. Through what are the Grass Roots' "Temptation Eyes" looking?
   a. a window
   b. their soul
   c. their hopes and dreams

4. The Grass Roots say "Let's Live for Today," while everyone else is chasing after what one thing?
   a. tomorrow
   b. dreams that can't come true
   c. the train of freedom

5. What is going to happen "Sooner or Later," according to the Grass Roots?
   a. the world will self-destruct
   b. you're gonna get caught foolin' around
   c. love is gonna get you

Grateful Dead

1. What did the Grateful Dead call themselves before turning to their immortal Dead moniker?
   a. Jerry and the Cycles
   b. the Bottom Step
   c. the Warlocks

2. Where did the Grateful Dead, along with the Jefferson Airplane, play in 1965 to commemorate opening day for this now legendary site?

    a. the Night Owl
    b. Fillmore West
    c. Grumman's Chinese Theater

3. What experience affected the Dead's early music, and won the group a different following?
    a. watching a Jimi Hendrix performance
    b. a religious conversion
    c. experimentation with LSD

4. On what famous San Francisco street did the Dead reside, amid the hippies and the drugs?
    a. Ashbury
    b. Haight
    c. Market Street

5. What was the Grateful Dead's only Top Twenty song?
    a. "Touch of Grey"
    b. "Truckin'"
    c. "Casey Jones"

Guess Who

1. The Guess Who's first hit, "Shakin' All Over," was actually released under a former name. What was it?
    a. B.C. and the Silverstones
    b. Chad Allan and the Expressions
    c. Randy and the Reflections

2. In "Laughing," what do the Guess Who say has happened to the best years?
    a. they've come and gone
    b. they have yet to come
    c. they're happening now

3. What do "These Eyes" of the Guess Who do every night for you?
    a. cry

    b. stay open

    c. dream about the future

4. The Guess Who tells their "American Woman" that they have more important things to do than spend their time doing what?

    a. growing old with her

    b. listening to her sob stories

    c. loving her

5. The Guess Who say in "No Time" that they are being summoned by what?

    a. a faraway star

    b. circuit court

    c. distant roads

Daryl Hall and John Oates

1. Daryl Hall and John Oates became the most successful duo in the history of rock, with more number one hits than any other rock two-some. Which duo did they surpass for this honor?

    a. the Everly Brothers

    b. Sonny and Cher

    c. Simon and Garfunkel

2. Of their six number one hits, which one stayed on top the longest for Daryl Hall and John Oates?

    a. "Maneater"

    b. "Kiss on My List"

    c. "Rich Girl"

3. In "One on One," what are Daryl Hall and John Oates here for?

    a. some rough-and-tumble action

    b. time out

    c. a chance to be alone

4. In "Say It Isn't So," what do Daryl Hall and John Oates say your first reaction is when things go bad?

    a. to blame them
    b. to call it quits
    c. to hide away

5. In "Sara Smile," although they say it's OK if you want to go, for how long do Daryl Hall and John Oates want you to stay?
    a. forever
    b. until tomorrow
    c. for another beer

Heart

1. Heart was shortened from their previous name. What was it?
    a. Broken Heart
    b. White Heart
    c. Heart and Soul

2. With whom did original Heart lead singer Ann Wilson duet in 1984 in a Top Ten hit?
    a. Mike Reno
    b. Michael McDonald
    c. Joe Cocker

3. In "Barracuda," what does Heart say will happen to you if the real thing doesn't do the trick?
    a. you're going to burn to the wick
    b. you'll lose your friends really quick
    c. you'll learn that love can make you sick

4. What is Heart listening to as they are "Alone"?
    a. the beating of their heart
    b. the empty silence
    c. the ticking of the clock

5. What did the "Magic Man" tell Heart with a smile?
    a. that he loves them

b. that he's hiding a secret from them

c. to come home

Jimi Hendrix

1. The Jimi Hendrix Experience opened for what band during their 1967 U.S. tour?
    a. the Monkees
    b. the Animals
    c. the Mamas and the Papas

2. What did Jimi Hendrix do during the 1967 Monterey Pop Festival performance that singled him out as a truly unique audience-pleaser?
    a. he set his guitar on fire
    b. he invited four spectators to join him on stage
    c. he played his electric guitar with his feet

3. What was the only song performed by Jimi Hendrix to break into the Top Forty rock charts?
    a. "Foxy Lady"
    b. "Purple Haze"
    c. "All Along the Watchtower"

4. According to Jimi Hendrix, what did the juggler say to the thief while they were "All Along the Watchtower"?
    a. that there must be some way out of here
    b. it's time to find more witnesses
    c. this is not the time to get caught

5. Because Jimi Hendrix is clouded by "Purple Haze," he doesn't know whether it's tomorrow or just _____.
    a. a very long today
    b. the end of time
    c. another yesterday

Herman's Hermits

1. How did Herman's Hermits get their name?

    a. the group members lived like hermits

    b. leader Peter Noone resembled googly-eyed Sherman on *The Bullwinkle Show*

    c. after a local female band, Merman's Mermaids

2. Which well-known guitarist actually helped in the recording of "I'm Into Something Good"?

    a. Jimmy Page

    b. Rick Derringer

    c. Paul McCartney

3. In what U.S. movie did Herman's Hermits make a cameo appearance while first visiting the states?

    a. *Freakout U.S.A.*

    b. *When the Boys Meet the Girls*

    c. *Bikini Beach Party*

4. In what year was their number one hit "I'm Henry VIII, I Am" written?

    a. 1911

    b. 1953

    c. 1962

5. In Herman's Hermits "I'm Henry VIII, I Am," Herman's wife won't marry a Willy or a _____.

    a. Sam

    b. Tom

    c. John

Hollies

1. How did the Hollies get their name?

    a. they were named during the Christmas season

    b. they were inspired by Buddy Holly

    c. they formed in Holland

2. Although popular in the UK long before breaking into the U.S. charts, what song finally launched their success in the states?

    a. "Bus Stop"
    b. "Carrie-Anne"
    c. "Look Through Any Window"

3. According to the Hollies in "Stop! Stop! Stop!" what does the dancing girl have on her fingers?

    a. rings
    b. mirrors
    c. cymbals

4. In the earliest games that the Hollies played with "Carrie-Anne," what role did they play?

    a. janitor
    b. teacher
    c. postman

5. How did the people stare at the Hollies and their friend as they waited at the "Bus Stop"?

    a. with envy and desire
    b. in horror and downright disbelief
    c. as if they were both quite insane

Tommy James and the Shondells

1. When did the name Shondells come to mind for Tommy James as a good name for his group?

    a. at his junior prom
    b. during a date with a girl named Shonda
    c. during study hall in the seventh grade

2. What inspired Tommy James to name his Top Five hit "Mony Mony"?

    a. an X-rated film
    b. his desperate need for money, money
    c. the Mutual of New York building

3. When we look over yonder in "Crystal Blue Persuasion," what do Tommy James and the Shondells say we'll see rising?

    a. new hopes and dreams
    b. two lovers in the dawn
    c. the sun

4. In "I Think We're Alone Now," what do the older people tell Tommy James and the Shondells when they are together with you?
    a. if they do anything, don't get caught
    b. to treat you with respect
    c. behave

5. Even though Tommy James and the Shondells hardly know the girl in "Crimson and Clover," what do they nevertheless feel they could do?
    a. kiss her
    b. love her
    c. dance with her

Jan and Dean

1. Jan and Dean's first hit, "Jennie Lee," was recorded under the moniker Jan and Arnie. Who was Jennie Lee and who was Arnie?
    a. Jennie Lee was a teacher; Arnie was Jan's brother
    b. Jennie Lee was a forties movie star; Arnie was Dean's alias
    c. Jennie Lee was a stripper; Arnie was a friend

2. "Linda," a hit for Jan and Dean in 1963, was written in the 1940s for a now well-known rocker. Who is she?
    a. Linda Ronstadt
    b. Belinda Carlisle
    c. Linda Eastman

3. What Beach Boys song did Dean Torrence sing lead on?
    a. "Sloop John B"
    b. "Fun, Fun, Fun"
    c. "Barbara Ann"

4. Only one Jan and Dean song ever reached number one. Which song was it?
   a. "Surf City"
   b. "The Little Old Lady (From Pasadena)"
   c. "Dead Man's Curve"

5. Just before Jan Berry crashed his Corvette and was nearly killed, what news had he received?
   a. he was accepted into UCLA
   b. his mom had died
   c. he got his draft notice

Jefferson Airplane

1. What is the significance of the name Jefferson Airplane?
   a. it was the name of a friend's dog
   b. it was a WWI fighter plane
   c. it combined their favorite president and mode of travel

2. Under what group name were their first hits, "Somebody to Love" and "White Rabbit," originally recorded?
   a. the Slick Stick
   b. the Where
   c. the Great Society

3. What two other group names stemmed from the original Jefferson Airplane?
   a. the Jets and Cloudburst
   b. Airplane and Concorde
   c. Jefferson Starship and Starship

4. What famous street corner is associated with the earliest days of the Jefferson Airplane?
   a. Hollywood and Vine
   b. Haight and Ashbury

   c. Sunset and Wilshire

5. In "White Rabbit," although one pill makes you smaller and one pill makes you tall, what do the Jefferson Airplane say happens with the pill your mother gives you?

   a. nothing

   b. it brings you the farthest away of all

   c. it drives you wild

Jethro Tull

1. After whom was the band Jethro Tull named?

   a. a lesser-known fifties actor

   b. an eighteenth-century agriculturalist

   c. the hero in a nineteenth-century novel

2. What on-stage eccentricity has made flutist Ian Anderson unique to the music world?

   a. he shakes uncontrollably during his performance

   b. he often plays while standing on one foot

   c. he plays the flute through his nose

3. Where does Jethro Tull say "Aqualung" is sitting?

   a. on the ocean bottom

   b. on a park bench

   c. in a hospital bed

4. In "Bungle in the Jungle," what does Jethro Tull say they scoff at?

   a. the monkeys

   b. people walking by

   c. elephants and rhinos

5. Because they enjoy "Living in the Past," Jethro Tull plans to go walking while others do what?

   a. shout of war's disaster

   b. run here and run there

c. sleep their life away

Elton John

1. What was Elton John's birth name?
   a. Paul Madrid
   b. Reginald Dwight
   c. Ian Brooks

2. After which famed blues singer (and his saxophonist) did he select the name Elton John?
   a. John Mayall
   b. Long John Baldry
   c. Johnny Mack

3. For whom was *Candle in the Wind* an ode?
   a. Jayne Mansfield
   b. Natalie Wood
   c. Marilyn Monroe

4. Which character did Elton John play in the Who's 1975 film version of the classic *Tommy*?
   a. Tommy's dad
   b. the Pinball Wizard
   c. Tommy

5. In "Philadelphia Freedom," what did Elton John do on the day he was born?
   a. he cried
   b. he swore he'd get out of this town
   c. he waved the flag

Journey

1. In what city was Journey formed?
   a. London
   b. New York City

    c. San Francisco

2. "Open Arms" was Journey's biggest single, charting at number two for six weeks. What song kept it from reaching the number one spot?

    a. "Centerfold"

    b. "Ebony and Ivory"

    c. "I Love Rock 'N Roll"

3. In "Open Arms," what does Journey ask about love?

    a. How could it be so blind?

    b. Why does it begin quickly but last so long?

    c. What is love all about?

4. When does Journey say you're "Lovin', Touchin', Squeezin'"?

    a. whenever the music's playing

    b. when they're all alone

    c. whenever you're near

5. When Journey says "Don't Stop Believin'," what do they tell you to do?

    a. hold on to that feeling

    b. reach for a star and never let go

    c. believe in the magic of rock and roll

Kinks

1. Who did the Kinks begin as, prior to their more popular name?

    a. the Beginners

    b. the Hedgehoppers

    c. the Ravens

2. What words in the original version of "Lola" had to be changed?

    a. "she made me a man"

    b. "girls will be boys and boys will be girls"

   c. "it tastes just like Coca-Cola"

3. What do the Kinks say the world of "A Well Respected Man" is built on?

   a. tradition
   b. secrecy
   c. punctuality

4. In "All Day and All of the Night," when is the only time that the Kinks feel all right?

   a. when they call you
   b. when they're by your side
   c. after a beer or two

5. In "Tired of Waiting for You," how were the Kinks before they met you?

   a. a lonely soul
   b. free
   c. always early

Kiss

1. In which country was Kiss leader Gene Simmons born?

   a. Israel
   b. Russia
   c. the USA

2. What unique rock and roll idea did each of the four members participate in during 1978?

   a. each hosted their own rock-radio talk show in different cities
   b. each released a solo album
   c. each sponsored a different commercial product on TV

3. In which album did Kiss first appear without the now famous Kiss makeup?

   a. *Kiss*

    b. *Kiss Unmasked*
    c. *Lick It Up*

4. In "I Was Made for Lovin' You," what does Kiss say you have that drives them wild?
    a. a bad attitude
    b. a sexy smile
    c. magic

5. Although "Christine Sixteen" has been around, what does Kiss add about her?
    a. she's nobody's fool
    b. she's young and clean
    c. she's never noticed them

Billy J. Kramer and the Dakotas

1. Which well-known manager signed Billy J. Kramer and the Dakotas to a multiyear contract?
    a. Tony Hatch
    b. Andrew Oldham
    c. Brian Epstein

2. Before he teamed up with the Dakotas, who was Billy J. Kramer's backup band?
    a. the Coasters
    b. the Flagstaffers
    c. the Pennsylvanians

3. Who penned three of the four hits sung by Billy J. Kramer and the Dakotas?
    a. John Lennon and Paul McCartney
    b. Mick Jagger and Keith Richards
    c. Eddie Holland, Lamont Dozier, and Brian Holland

4. According to Billy J. Kramer and the Dakotas in "Bad to Me," why won't the birds in the sky be sad and lonely?
    a. the sun is shining bright

   b. they're together with their girlfriend
   c. there's love in the air

5. What can't Billy J. Kramer and the Dakotas do with you when they're ready to, because of the "Little Children" hanging around?
   a. tie you up and light a fire
   b. turn the lights down low
   c. kiss you

Led Zeppelin

1. Which group's members suggested the name Led Zeppelin?
   a. the Who
   b. the Yardbirds
   c. Cream

2. On what TV show did Led Zeppelin make its U.S. debut?
   a. *The Midnight Special*
   b. *Don Kirschner's Rock Concert*
   c. *The Sonny and Cher Show*

3. What label did Led Zeppelin form in 1974?
   a. Big Tree
   b. Swan Song
   c. Casablanca

4. Which classic Led Zeppelin song was never released as a single?
   a. "D'yer Mak'er"
   b. "Whole Lotta Love"
   c. "Stairway to Heaven"

5. Because they've got a "Whole Lotta Love," what does Led Zeppelin want to be for you?
   a. a backdoor man
   b. your butler

   c. your number one

John Lennon

1. What was the name of the album in which John Lennon and Yoko Ono posed nude for the cover?
   a. *Some Time in New York City*
   b. *Live Peace in Toronto*
   c. *Two Virgins*

2. What was John Lennon's last single to reach the Top Five in the music charts?
   a. "Woman"
   b. "Whatever Gets You Through the Night"
   c. "(Just Like) Starting Over"

3. John Lennon asks if you can "Imagine" all the people doing what?
   a. living life in peace
   b. banning all the guns
   c. drowning in the sea of love

4. In "Instant Karma (We All Shine On)," what does John Lennon say that you are?
   a. a superstar
   b. a dreamer
   c. a ray of hope on a cloudy day

5. What does John Lennon say his "Woman" understands?
   a. how to make a man beg
   b. the little child inside the man
   c. little things only a woman can

Gary Lewis and the Playboys

1. What incident halted the success of Gary Lewis and the Playboys?

   a. when Gary's father, Jerry, started the MDA telethon

   b. when Gary Lewis was drafted

   c. the British Invasion

2. Because they want you to "Save Your Heart for Me," what do Gary Lewis and the Playboys ask you not to do when you're dancing under starlit skies?

   a. think of fifty ways to say goodbye

   b. think you're God's gift and start acting wise

   c. let the stars get in your eyes

3. In "Count Me In," Gary Lewis and the Playboys say that if you count the ones who've doubted you, _____.

   a. count them out

   b. they're first on the list

   c. you'll need a calculator

4. Gary Lewis and the Playboys say that "This Diamond Ring" can be something beautiful under what condition?

   a. if there's love behind it

   b. if you pawn it at the perfect time

   c. if there's a girl to give it to

5. In "Sure Gonna Miss Her," what is it that Gary Lewis and the Playboys never said until they found out it was too late to say?

   a. they love you

   b. they were sorry

   c. goodbye

Lovin' Spoonful

1 Before forming the Lovin' Spoonful, two members belonged to a group with members who later formed another top sixties group. Who was this other group?

   a. the Byrds

   b. Creedence Clearwater Revival

   c. the Mamas and the Papas

2. In what Francis Ford Coppola movie did "Darling Be Home Soon" appear?
   a. *Younger Generation*
   b. *What's Up Tiger Lily?*
   c. *You're a Big Boy Now*

3. For what television show in the seventies did leader John Sebastian sing the theme song?
   a. *The Jeffersons*
   b. *Welcome Back, Kotter*
   c. *The Love Boat*

4. Why do the Lovin' Spoonful say that "You Didn't Have to Be So Nice"?
   a. they would have liked you anyway
   b. they were already going steady
   c. they were looking for a bad girl

5. In "Summer in the City," the Lovin' Spoonful depict themselves as a cool cat looking for _____.
   a. a hot time
   b. a kitty
   c. a slow rat

Lynyrd Skynyrd

1. How did Lynyrd Skynyrd get their name?
   a. it was an abbreviated name for two bands, Sky Lion and the Byrds
   b. they named themselves after a gym teacher
   c. a local deejay suggested it during an early performance

2. In "Sweet Home Alabama," who did Lynyrd Skynyrd lambaste as being no friend to the South?
   a. Richard Nixon

    b. Neil Young

    c. George Wallace

3. What album featured the band in flames, as if presaging their fateful crash?

    a. *Street Survivors*

    b. *One More for the Road*

    c. *Free at Last*

4. In "Free Bird," what does Lynyrd Skynyrd wonder, if they left tomorrow?

    a. Would you still remember them?

    b. Would tomorrow ever come?

    c. Would it cause them future sorrow?

5. In "What's Your Name?," what city is Lynyrd Skynyrd in?

    a. Memphis

    b. Tucson

    c. Boise

The Mamas and the Papas

1. Before joining the Mamas and the Papas, what was Mama Cass working as?

    a. an actress

    b. a waitress

    c. a teacher

2. Which song by the Mamas and the Papas tells the story of their rise to rock stardom?

    a. "Creeque Alley"

    b. "Monday, Monday"

    c. "California Dreamin'"

3. What was the Mamas and the Papas' only number one hit?

    a. "Dedicated to the One I Love"

   b. "Monday, Monday"
   c. "California Dreamin'"

4. In "Words of Love," what do the Mamas and the Papas say you must do to win a girl's heart?
   a. send her somewhere she's never been
   b. flash lots of money
   c. fight for her affection

5. In "Dedicated to the One I Love," what do the Mamas and the Papas need you to do for them while they are far away?
   a. write to them every day
   b. pray
   c. leave on your love light

Manfred Mann

1. Who was the lead singer of the band Manfred Mann?
   a. Manfred Mann
   b. Mike Hugg
   c. Paul Jones

2. Which Top Ten Manfred Mann hit was written by Bob Dylan, inspired by a movie?
   a. "Do Wah Diddy Diddy"
   b. "With God on Our Side"
   c. "The Mighty Quinn"

3. Which song by Manfred Man's Earth Band was written by Bruce Springsteen?
   a. "Spirit in the Night"
   b. "Runner"
   c. "Blinded by the Light"

4. In "Do Wah Diddy Diddy," what did Manfred Mann and their girlfriend do after they walked to their door?
   a. they slapped each other silly

   b. they kissed a little more

   c. they made romance

5. According to Manfred Mann, how is everybody feeling before "The Mighty Quinn" makes his appearance?

   a. in despair

   b. excited

   c. bored

Paul McCartney (and Wings)

1. What was their first Top Five hit recorded as Paul McCartney and Wings?

   a. "Live and Let Die"

   b. "Band on the Run"

   c. "My Love"

2. What was the inspiration behind "Jet"?

   a. McCartney's pet

   b. a recent love gone sour

   c. the British Concorde

3. What song did Wings member Denny Laine sing lead on, a 1965 hit for a legendary British group he helped form?

   a. "Double Shot (of My Baby's Love)"

   b. "She's Not There"

   c. "Go Now"

4. What song was written for McCartney's wife when she was just a baby?

   a. "My Eyes Adored You"

   b. "Linda"

   c. "Angel Eyes"

5. Of the nine number one hits by McCartney (as a solo, in a duet, and with Wings), which stayed on the top for the longest?

   a. "Ebony and Ivory"

    b. "Silly Love Songs"

    c. "Say Say Say"

John Cougar Mellencamp

1. The manager of what British rock megastar first signed John Cougar to a record contract?

    a. Elton John

    b. Rod Stewart

    c. David Bowie

2. What tribute to the American way of life was John Cougar Mellencamp's only number one hit?

    a. "R.O.C.K. in the U.S.A."

    b. "Jack and Diane"

    c. "Pink Houses"

3. In "Hurts So Good," what does John Cougar long for now that he's getting older?

    a. a home and a family

    b. painkillers and a girl to call his own

    c. those young boy days

4. According to John Cougar Mellencamp, when did the girl's dreams burn up like "Paper in Fire"?

    a. when she was left for another

    b. when life passed her by and left her sinking in despair

    c. when she got too close to her expectations

5. Where does John Cougar say "Jack and Diane" are growing up?

    a. in the heartland of America

    b. down in the boondocks and the ghettos

    c. in a lover's paradise

Men at Work

1. From what country did Men at Work originate?

    a. England
    b. South Africa
    c. Australia

2. *Business As Usual* topped the U.S. charts for fifteen weeks, surpassing by three weeks the previous highest-ranking debut album. Who held the previous record?

    a. the Beatles
    b. the Supremes
    c. the Monkees

3. Which of the following was *not* a hit from their first album?

    a. "Overkill"
    b. "Who Can It Be Now?"
    c. "Down Under"

4. In "Who Can It Be Now?" what do Men at Work say to the person who is knocking at their door?

    a. they've already given their broken heart away
    b. nobody's home
    c. go away and don't come around there anymore

5. In "Down Under," how tall was the man Men at Work met from Brazil?

    a. 5'10"
    b. 6'4"
    c. 6'1"

Steve Miller Band

1. From what renowned band leader did Steve Miller receive his first guitar lesson?

    a. Glenn Miller
    b. Mitch Miller
    c. Les Paul

2. While in high school, Steve Miller formed his first band, the Marksmen Combo, which included another future star, who in fact learned the guitar from Miller. Who was this friend?

    a. Eddie Van Halen
    b. Richie Sambora
    c. Boz Scaggs

3. According to the Steve Miller Band in "Take the Money and Run," where did Billy Joe and Bobby Sue head once they decided to cut loose from their uneventful life?

    a. El Paso
    b. Mexico
    c. Quebec

4. In "Abracadabra," what happens to the Steve Miller Band when you call their name?

    a. you make them go insane
    b. they heat up like a burning flame
    c. they long to go to from where they came

5. What kind of airplane is the Steve Miller Band's "Jet Airliner"?

    a. DC7
    b. 747
    c. 707

Monkees

1. In what newspaper did an ad appear seeking four guys to form the Monkees?

    a. *Rolling Stone*
    b. *Wall Street Journal*
    c. *Daily Variety*

2. Which of the following did *not* try out for (and get turned down for) the Monkees?

    a. Glen Campbell

   b. Stephen Stills

   c. Charles Manson

3. In what Broadway musical did Davy Jones perform before becoming a Monkee?

   a. *Jesus Christ Superstar*

   b. *Oliver*

   c. *West Side Story*

4. In what TV series did Mickey Dolenz appear as a youngster?

   a. *Gilligan's Island*

   b. *Ben Casey*

   c. *Circus Boy*

5. Although other people say in "Hey, Hey, We're the Monkees" that the prefab foursome just want to cause problems by monkeying around, how do the Monkees respond?

   a. they're just normal people who like hanging upside down

   b. that's what they're here for, but don't let that get you down

   c. they're too busy singing to put anybody down

Moody Blues

1. What was the Moody Blues' first Top Twenty hit?

   a. "Go Now"

   b. "Tuesday Afternoon (Forever Afternoon)"

   c. "Question"

2. What was the name of the Moody Blues' own label, started in 1969?

   a. Threshold

   b. Deram

   c. Virgin

3. Which song was recorded in 1968, then released as a single in 1972 and rereleased in 1978?

    a. "Your Wildest Dreams"
    b. "The Story in Your Eyes"
    c. "Nights in White Satin"

4. According to the Moody Blues in "Your Wildest Dreams," what was theirs beneath the stars?
    a. the universe
    b. your love
    c. money and fancy cars

5. In "The Love That's Deep Within You," what do the Moody Blues say we're part of?
    a. a cosmic field of energy
    b. a never-ending circle of love
    c. the fire that is burning

Van Morrison

1. In what country was George Ivan (Van) Morrison born?
    a. Russia
    b. Northern Ireland
    c. Scotland

2. What rock classic did Van Morrison write and then record with his sixties band?
    a. "Fever"
    b. "Gloria"
    c. "Louie Louie"

3. Where did Van Morrison and his "Brown-Eyed Girl" go when the rains came?
    a. to his room
    b. down in the hollow
    c. into the classroom

4. In "Domino," what does Van Morrison think it's time for?
    a. a change

   b. playing games

   c. making love

5. In "Moondance," what does Van Morrison say it's a fantabulous night to do?

   a. make romance

   b. go driving under the stars

   c. let it all hang loose and go dancing

Tom Petty and the Heartbreakers

1. What movie is said to have been the inspiration for Tom Petty's musical direction?

   a. *Rebel Without a Cause*

   b. *Follow That Dream*

   c. *2001: A Space Odyssey*

2. What was the band's first hit to reach the Top Ten spot?

   a. "The Waiting"

   b. "Refugee"

   c. "Don't Do Me Like That"

3. What major rock figure did Tom Petty and the Heartbreakers back up during 1986–87?

   a. Bob Dylan

   b. Bob Seger

   c. Richard Marx

4. In "Here Comes My Girl," what word do Tom Petty and the Heartbreakers use to describe the town when their girl isn't around?

   a. boring

   b. hopeless

   c. exciting

5. Because you're living like a "Refugee," what do Tom Petty and the Heartbreakers say must have happened when you were young?

    a. you must have dropped out of school
    b. somebody must have kicked you around
    c. you must have given up on the power of love

Pink Floyd

1. How did Pink Floyd get its name?
    a. after the "Pink Panther" cartoon
    b. after two blues singers
    c. after the sixties hit album *Music From Big Pink*, by the Band

2. In what year did Pink Floyd first begin appearing as regulars in London Nightclubs?
    a. 1966
    b. 1970
    c. 1973

3. "Another Brick in the Wall (Part II)" was their biggest hit, hitting number one for four weeks. What was their only other Top Forty hit?
    a. "Money"
    b. "Echoes"
    c. "Run Like Hell"

4. In what 1970 movie soundtrack did Pink Floyd include three songs?
    a. *Jesus Christ Superstar*
    b. *Zabriskie Point*
    c. *Butch Cassidy and the Sundance Kid*

5. Which album defied gravity by staying on the album charts for over *ten* years?
    a. *The Wall*
    b. *Dark Side of the Moon*
    c. *Ummagumma*

Police

1. Who inspired the name for the Police?
   a. Randy California, in his song "1984"
   b. Stewart Copeland's father
   c. George Harrison

2. What motivated Gordon Sumner to adopt the nickname Sting?
   a. Andy Summers' pet snake
   b. a favorite black and yellow jersey
   c. his raspy voice

3. Which Police album reigned at number one for seventeen weeks and spawned a number one single?
   a. *Syncronicity*
   b. *Zenyatta Mondatta*
   c. *Ghost in the Machine*

4. What product did the Police promote in a 1978 television ad?
   a. Levi's jeans
   b. Nike shoes
   c. Wrigley's gum

5. In "Every Breath You Take," since what event have the Police been lost without a trace?
   a. since you stole their breath away
   b. since you blinded them with your love
   c. since you've gone

Pretenders

1. How did the band get the name Pretenders?
   a. rock fans thought they weren't really singing their songs
   b. from the fifties hit "The Great Pretender"

    c. by picking a word at random from the dictionary

2. In what movie did the Pretenders' biggest hit, "Back on the Chain Gang," appear?

    a. *The Goonies*

    b. *The King of Comedy*

    c. *Two of a Kind*

3. In "Back on the Chain Gang," what did the Pretenders find that reminded them of the happiest days of their life?

    a. an old 45 rpm record

    b. a picture of you

    c. their high school diary

4. In "Brass in Pocket (I'm Special)," what do the Pretenders want to get from you?

    a. your clothes

    b. your attention

    c. a commitment

5. What do the Pretenders say the "Middle of the Road" is trying to do?

    a. split them in two

    b. keep them from losing you

    c. find them

Procol Harum

1. What inspired Procol Harum to select their group name?

    a. the Vienna Boys Choir

    b. a label on a designer shirt

    c. a friend's Siamese cat

2. What award did "A Whiter Shade of Pale" win in 1977?

    a. A Best Arrangement Grammy award

    b. *Rolling Stone*'s underground gold record distinction

   c. Best British Pop Single 1952–77 award

3. On what melody is Procol Harum's classic hit "A Whiter Shade of Pale" based?

   a. *Bolero*
   b. *Francesca da Rimini*
   c. *Sleepers Awake*

4. In "A Whiter Shade of Pale," what did Procol Harum do across the floor?

   a. dance
   b. throw a chair
   c. turn cartwheels

5. In "Conquistador," what does Procol Harum hope to find?

   a. a place to unwind
   b. a lady in waiting
   c. uncharted lands and desert sands

Gary Puckett and the Union Gap

1. Gary Puckett was born in Hibbing, Minnesota. What legendary rock figure had his earliest roots in that area?

   a. Chuck Berry
   b. Elvis Presley
   c. Bob Dylan

2. In which state is Union Gap?

   a. New York
   b. Pennsylvania
   c. Washington

3. What do Gary Puckett and the Union Gap accusingly ask their "Woman, Woman"?

   a. Did you see my wallet around?
   b. Have you got cheating on your mind?

    c. Where were you when I called last night?

4. According to Gary Puckett and the Union Gap, "This Girl Is a Woman Now" who has found out what it's all about and she's learning to _____.

    a. deceive
    b. live
    c. love

5. What are Gary Puckett and the Union Gap losing "Over You"?

    a. weight
    b. sleep
    c. their sanity

Queen

1. In what country was Queen leader Freddy Mercury born?

    a. Austria
    b. Tanzania
    c. Australia

2. What Queen single not only topped the U.S. rock charts but also hit number two on the R and B charts as well?

    a. "Crazy Little Thing Called Love"
    b. "We Are the Champions/We Will Rock You"
    c. "Another One Bites the Dust"

3. For what 1980 movie did Queen write and provide the soundtrack?

    a. *Flash Gordon*
    b. *Urban Cowboy*
    c. *One-Trick Pony*

4. In "Bohemian Rhapsody," how does Queen describe itself?

    a. as lovers without a song

    b. as easy come, easy go

    c. rough as a leather whip

5. In "We Are the Champions," what does Queen consider itself the champion of?

    a. the world

    b. your love

    c. their destiny

REO Speedwagon

1. REO Speedwagon got their name after Ransom Eli Olds. Who was he?

    a. a 1920s blues singer

    b. the father of the Oldsmobile Corporation

    c. Kevin Cronin's great-grandfather

2. *Hi Infidelity* broke REO Speedwagon into the top of the album charts and included such hits as "Keep On Loving You" and "Take It on the Run." Which album was this for the band?

    a. their first

    b. their third

    c. their eleventh

3. "Keep On Loving You" was REO Speedwagon's first number one hit. What was their other number one song?

    a. "Can't Fight This Feeling"

    b. "Take It on the Run"

    c. "Keep the Fire Burnin'"

4. In "Keep On Loving You," what does REO Speedwagon say you should have noticed by the look in their eyes?

    a. they were blindly in love with you

    b. there was something missing

    c. they could see right through you

5. If you "Take It on the Run," then what does REO Speedwagon say they don't want?

   a. to buy a home
   b. to be a one-trick pony
   c. for you to be around

Paul Revere and the Raiders

1. Who was the lead singer of Paul Revere and the Raiders?
   a. Paul Revere
   b. Freddy Weller
   c. Mark Lindsay

2. What television music show, produced by Dick Clark, did Paul Revere and the Raiders host from 1968 to 1969?
   a. *Shindig*
   b. *Where the Action Is*
   c. *Happening '68*

3. What was the band's only number one hit?
   a. "Good Thing"
   b. "Indian Reservation"
   c. "Kicks"

4. After Paul Revere and the Raiders are through showing you their "Good Thing," what do they say you'll feel it seems right to do?
   a. have them stay there tonight
   b. never say goodbye
   c. leave all your other boyfriends behind

5. According to the Raiders, the residents on their "Indian Reservation" are so proud to do what two things?
   a. remain free and prosper
   b. be treated fairly and employed equally
   c. live and die

Rolling Stones

1. The Rolling Stones' name was taken from a Muddy Waters song. Who first suggested the name?
   a. Muddy Waters
   b. Brian Jones
   c. John Lennon

2. Before leading the Rolling Stones, what band did Mick Jagger sing for?
   a. Blues Incorporated
   b. the London Boys
   c. the Edge of Tyme

3. On what television show did the Rolling Stones make their U.S. debut appearance?
   a. *The Ed Sullivan Show*
   b. *The Tonight Show*
   c. *The Les Crane Show*

4. "(I Can't Get No) Satisfaction" was the Stones' first number one hit. What was their last?
   a. "Start Me Up"
   b. "Honky Tonk Woman"
   c. "Miss You"

5. What never-released 1968 television show featured performances by Eric Clapton, the Who, and John Lennon, along with the Stones?
   a. *Sympathy for the Devil*
   b. *Up Close: The 1969 U.K. Music Scene*
   c. *Rock and Roll Circus*

6. What underground classic did the Rolling Stones record (but never release) to complete a contract deal with Decca records?
   a. "Hold On Cocaine"
   b. "Decca the Halls"
   c. "Cocksucker Blues"

7. At which Rolling Stones concert did the Hell's Angels serve as security?
   a. Hyde Park
   b. Asbury Park
   c. Altamont

8. In what 1970 film did Mick Jagger act as a lipstick-wearing, retired rock star?
   a. *Gimmie Shelter*
   b. *Performance*
   c. *It's Only Rock 'n' Roll*

9. Which Rolling Stones album featured a 3-D cover?
   a. *Beggar's Banquet*
   b. *Sticky Fingers*
   c. *Their Satanic Majesties Request*

10. What time is it that the Rolling Stones say is the perfect time for a "Street Fighting Man"?
   a. whenever the cause is right
   b. summer
   c. when the sun goes down

11. Even though "Ruby Tuesday" can't be chained down, what do the Stones add?
   a. they're still going to miss her
   b. they've got the rope just in case
   c. they'd like to be chained down anytime

12. In "The Last Time," what did the Rolling Stones say they told their girlfriend once and then twice?
   a. she never listens to their advice
   b. she's the sugar of their spice
   c. she has a heart as cold as ice

13. Although they have their girl "Under My Thumb," what can the Rolling Stones still do?
   a. play the guitar without losing a beat
   b. look at someone else

    c. be her best friend

14. According to the Rolling Stones in "Play With Fire," where does your mother own a block?

    a. in St. John's Wood
    b. in Gloucestershire
    c. in hell

15. The Rolling Stones never stopped "Reelin' and Rockin'" until what went down?

    a. the roof
    b. the moon
    c. the shades

16. According to the Rolling Stones, what will "Not Fade Away"?

    a. lipstick on their collar
    b. the stains from a broken heart
    c. love that's love

17. In "Have You Seen Your Mother, Baby," what are the Rolling Stones glad they helped you do?

    a. open your eyes
    b. become reunited
    c. break free

18. In "Time Is on My Side," what kind of love do the Rolling Stones say they can offer you?

    a. love with a money-back guarantee
    b. the half-hour kind
    c. real love

19. What do the Rolling Stones tell "Angie"?

    a. no one can say they didn't try
    b. she's the girl they've always dreamed of
    c. they're free to do whatever they want any old time

20. In "Start Me Up," what do the Rolling Stones say you make a grown man do?

    a. cry

   b. beg

   c. leave their thoughts behind

Mitch Ryder and the Detroit Wheels

1. What were Mitch Ryder and the Detroit Wheels originally known as?

   a. the Memphis Experiment

   b. Billy Lee and the Rivieras

   c. the Manhattan Dimension

2. What was Mitch Ryder's birth name?

   a. William Levise Jr.

   b. Conrad Mitchell Rydell

   c. Mitchell Ryder Bernstein

3. What little-known song, recorded without Mitch Ryder in the late sixties, was a tribute to a psychedelic drug?

   a. "Pushin' Up"

   b. "Linda Sue Dixon"

   c. "Living in Ecstasy"

4. In "C. C. Rider," when do Mitch Ryder and the Detroit Wheels say they will be returning once they leave?

   a. next summer

   b. in the fall

   c. in a month or two

5. What is the name of Mitch Ryder and the Detroit Wheels' "Devil With a Blue Dress On"?

   a. Molly

   b. Jenny

   c. Sally

Searchers

1. From what did the Searchers select their group name?

    a. a movie
    b. a TV game show
    c. a novel

2. The Searchers' first drummer, Norman McGarry, left the group to join the band Rory Storm and the Hurricanes, replacing their drummer, who had also switched groups. Which drummer did McGarry replace?
    a. Keith Moon
    b. Ringo Starr
    c. Charlie Watts

3. Who cowrote the Searchers' first U.S. hit, "Needles and Pins," with Jack Nitzsche?
    a. Sonny Bono
    b. Del Shannon
    c. Paul Simon

4. How many bottles of "Love Potion Number Nine" did the Searchers see when they sought to make a purchase?
    a. nine
    b. seven
    c. one

5. In "Needles and Pins," what do the Searchers say their girlfriend will one day learn to do?
    a. get down on her knees
    b. be their only love
    c. sew

Bob Seger and the Silver Bullet Band

1. What was the name of Bob Seger's band during the time of "Ramblin' Gamblin' Man"?
    a. Bob Seger and the Last Heard
    b. Bob Seger System

    c. the Quaker City Boys

2. What famous sixties rocker became an early publisher of Bob Seger's songs?
   a. Del Shannon
   b. Lou Christie
   c. Tommy Roe

3. For what album did Bob Seger win Best Rock Performance at the 1981 Grammy awards?
   a. *Stranger in Town*
   b. *Night Moves*
   c. *Against the Wind*

4. What do Bob Seger and the Silver Bullet Band say "Old Time Rock and Roll" has that today's music doesn't have?
   a. the same soul
   b. a message in the lines
   c. a rockin' beat

5. Although he's older now, what is Bob Seger still doing "Against the Wind"?
   a. running
   b. standing tall
   c. spitting

Bruce Springsteen

1. What was the name of Bruce Springsteen's long-running backup group?
   a. the Sonic Boom
   b. the E Street Band
   c. the Asbury Dukes

2. Bruce Springsteen never had a U.S. number one hit single. Which song reached number two?
   a. "Born in the U.S.A."

    b. "Dancing in the Dark"
    c. "Hungry Heart"

3. Springsteen rejected a $12 million offer to promote which company?
    a. Exxon
    b. Budweiser
    c. Chrysler

4. What nickname has stuck with Bruce Springsteen through the years?
    a. the Asbury Prince
    b. the Gunslinger
    c. the Boss

5. Which of the following hits did Springsteen *not* write?
    a. "Island Girl"/Elton John
    b. "Fire"/Pointer Sisters
    c. "Blinded by the Light"/Manfred Mann's Earth Band

6. What famous early sixties star did Springsteen produce during the early eighties?
    a. Ben E. King
    b. Roy Orbison
    c. Gary U.S. Bonds

7. In "Born in the U.S.A.," what does Bruce Springsteen say you'll do after being kicked around and beat too much?
    a. get even with the rest of the world until they've had enough
    b. spend half your life covering it up
    c. learn to take it as a way to grow tough

8. How old was Bruce Springsteen in "My Hometown" when he went running to pick up a newspaper for his dad?
    a. thirteen
    b. twenty-four

   c. eight

9. Because you and he were "Born to Run," what does Bruce Springsteen call you two?

   a. asphalt athletes

   b. birds of a feather

   c. tramps

10. In "Hungry Heart," what did Bruce Springsteen do when he went out for a ride?

   a. he took you along

   b. he headed for your place

   c. he never went back

Steely Dan

1. How did Steely Dan leaders Donald Fagen and Walter Becker first meet?

   a. while competing in a music talent show

   b. from an encounter during a high school football game

   c. through an ad

2. With what sixties band did Donald Fagen help out as a backup keyboardist and vocalist?

   a. the Turtles

   b. Iron Butterfly

   c. Jay and the Americans

3. What is a "Steely Dan"?

   a. a reinforced support beam, used in commercial buildings

   b. a type of marble

   c. a steam-powered dildo

4. According to Steely Dan in "Hey Nineteen," for which group have hard times fallen?

   a. the Beatles

   b. the Soul Survivors

   c. hippies and flower children

5. What instrument does Steely Dan plan to learn in "Deacon Blues," so they can play it just how they feel?

   a. violin

   b. tuba

   c. saxophone

Steppenwolf

1. What inspired Steppenwolf's producer in naming the band?

   a. a German fairy tale

   b. the name of one of Jupiter's moons

   c. a novel

2. In which two 1969 films did Steppenwolf songs appear?

   a. *People* and *The Games*

   b. *Midnight Cowboy* and *Woodstock*

   c. *Candy* and *Easy Rider*

3. In which Steppenwolf song were the now legendary words "heavy metal" originally found?

   a. "Magic Carpet Ride"

   b. "Sookie Sookie"

   c. "Born to Be Wild"

4. According to Steppenwolf in "Magic Carpet Ride," what will set you free?

   a. the magic carpet

   b. the sounds of the music

   c. the fantasy

5. Steppenwolf wants to damn "The Pusher" because they've seen too many people walking around with __.

   a. tombstones in their eyes

   b. murder in their hearts

c.   dreams that can't come true

Rod Stewart

1. What top British band of the late sixties was Rod Stewart *not* a member of?
  a. the Hollies
  b. the Faces
  c. the Jeff Beck Group

2. What professional sport did Rod Stewart seriously pursue, though his talents in music proved greater?
  a. soccer
  b. tennis
  c. golf

3. Which number one U.S. hit was generally banned in the UK?
  a. "Tonight's the Night (Gonna Be Alright)"
  b. "Da Ya Think I'm Sexy"
  c. "Hot Legs"

4. What does Rod Stewart tell the "Young Turks"?
  a. that America is for the free
  b. that time is on their side
  c. to stay away from his front door

5. In which month is Rod Stewart singing about "Maggie May"?
  a. December
  b. May
  c. September

Supertramp

1. From what did the British band get its name?
  a. a dredging rig

   b. a book

   c. the movies *Superman* and *Lady and the Tramp*

2. Whose sponsorship of the group helped Supertramp get its start?

   a. the British government

   b. a young Dutch millionaire

   c. an oil company

3. Which of the following was their highest-charting hit?

   a. "Give a Little Bit"

   b. "Take the Long Way Home"

   c. "The Logical Song"

4. In "Goodbye Stranger," what does Supertramp say they hope you find?

   a. a new friend

   b. your paradise

   c. someone who will share their love with you

5. In "The Logical Song," what does Supertramp say life seemed like when they were young?

   a. a ball of confusion

   b. a wonderful miracle

   c. a never-ending picnic

10cc

1. 10cc was named by British music-industry giant Jonathan King. Which of the following groups did he also name?

   a. Genesis

   b. Thompson Twins

   c. Depeche Mode

2. With what top sixties British band did 10cc singer-guitarist Eric Stewart play?

   a. Manfred Mann

   b. Gerry and the Pacemakers

   c. Wayne Fontana and the Mindbenders

3. Before they became 10cc, the group (then a trio, later to add a fourth member and become 10cc) had a Top Forty U.S. hit (Top Five in the UK) What was this hit?

   a. "Telstar"

   b. "Psychotic Reaction"

   c. "Neanderthal Man"

4. In "The Things We Do for Love," what does 10cc say is happening to too many broken hearts?

   a. they're falling in the river

   b. they're hanging on to dreams that can't come true

   c. they're giving up too soon

5. 10cc says "I'm Not in Love," so how do they explain how they feel?

   a. you've got them under your spell

   b. love and hate are just two of a kind

   c. it's just a phase they're going through

Three Dog Night

1. What is the origin of the name Three Dog Night?

   a. it's a takeoff on the Beatles' movie *A Hard Day's Night*

   b. it's the name of their first gig, a coffeehouse nightclub

   c. it's an Australian term for a very cold night

2. For which group did Three Dog Night leader Danny Hutton audition unsuccessfully before forming his new band?

   a. the Monkees

   b. the Standells

   c. the Grass Roots

3. Who wrote their biggest hit, "Joy to the World"?

    a. Randy Newman
    b. Harry Nilsson
    c. Hoyt Axton

4. What will Three Dog Night wash away with the rain in "Shambala"?
    a. your perfume and lipstick
    b. .their trouble and pain
    c. acne and lice

5. According to Three Dog Night, what number is the next loneliest besides "One"?
    a. one-half
    b. zero
    c. two

Toto

1. The origin of the group name Toto has been an enduring mystery. Which of the following was *not* a reason for the band's choice of their name?
    a. "Toto" is an easy-to-remember word with many meanings
    b. it was inspired by *The Wizard of Oz*
    c. it came from lead singer Bobby Kimball's original last name, Toteaux

2. For what TV theme-song composition did Toto member David Paich and his father win an Emmy?
    a. "Welcome Back, Kotter"
    b. "Ironside"
    c. "Hill Street Blues"

3. How many Grammy awards did Toto win in 1983?
    a. two
    b. three
    c. six

4. What is the only thing Toto wants to do to "Rosanna" in the middle of the night?

   a. hold her tight
   b. see her eyes
   c. leave her sight

5. In "Africa," what does Toto hear echoing tonight?
   a. thunder
   b. your voice
   c. drums

Troggs

1. The Troggs shortened their original name, the Troglodytes. What is a troglodyte?
   a. a mythical caveman
   b. a small but voracious rodent
   c. a dental drill

2. From what country did the Troggs come?
   a. Canada
   b. Holland
   c. England

3. In what parts of their bodies do the Troggs feel that "Love Is All Around"?
   a. heart and tummy
   b. fingers and toes
   c. ears and nose

4. What do the Troggs want "With a Girl Like You"?
   a. to spend their life with you
   b. to take you everywhere they go
   c. to have you under their skin

5. According to the Troggs, how does their "Wild Thing" make everything?
   a. trippy
   b. crazy
   c. groovy

Turtles

1. Which of the following were the Turtles *not* known as?
    a. the Nightriders
    b. the Undivided Sum
    c. the Crossfires

2. The Turtles' name was originally suggested to be spelled differently. How did their manager want it spelled, and why?
    a. Turttles, to match the original spelling of the Beatles' name (Beattles)
    b. Tyrtles, to imitate the Byrds' spelling
    c. Turdles, to make fun of the pop music trends

3. With which record label did the Turtles record all their sixties hits?
    a. White Whale
    b. ABC-Paramount
    c. Jubilee

4. In which film, produced and starring an icon in rock satire, did leaders Howard Kaylan and Mark Volman appear in 1971?
    a. *The Man Who Fell to Earth*
    b. *Gator*
    c. *200 Motels*

5. In "It Ain't Me Babe," where do the Turtles want you to go?
    a. away from their window
    b. to the dance Saturday night
    c. to your new boyfriend

Van Halen

1. In what country were the Van Halen brothers born?
    a. Holland

   b. France

   c. the USA

2. Who replaced lead singer David Lee Roth shortly after his departure from Van Halen?

   a. Jon Bon Jovi

   b. Alex Van Halen

   c. Sammy Hagar

3. For what pop megastar did Eddie Van Halen contribute a guitar solo?

   a. Michael Jackson

   b. Paul Simon

   c. Madonna

4. What actress did Eddie Van Halen marry in 1981?

   a. Vanna White

   b. Valerie Bertinelli

   c. Susan Sarandon

5. In "Dance the Night Away," what does Van Halen call the feeling they have?

   a. a fine and natural sight

   b. love in the third degree

   c. the feeling of freedom and fun

Who

1. Why did the Who abandon their original group name, the High Numbers?

   a. it associated the band with drugs

   b. the name was considered too long

   c. "High Numbers" sounded too much like gambling

2. What stage antic became a Who trademark?

   a. setting fire to their equipment

   b. tossing a large rubber ball into the audience

   c. smashing their guitars

3. In what world-televised live recording session did
    drummer Keith Moon perform in 1967?
    a. the Rolling Stones' Royal Albert Hall performance
    b. *The 1967 Grammy Awards*, with the Yardbirds
    c. the Beatles' *All You Need Is Love*

4. What was the name of the 1979 documentary film on
    the Who?
    a. *The Kids Are Alright*
    b. *Tommy*
    c. *Quadrophenia*

5. Keith Moon died in the same apartment that another
    famous rocker had died in four years prior. Who was
    that star?
    a. Mama Cass Elliot
    b. Brian Jones
    c. Eddie Cochran

Edgar Winter Group

1. What did the Edgar Winter Group originally call
    themselves?
    a. White Trash
    b. Pigmentosa Nervosa
    c. the Blues Experiment

2. What unusual physical characteristic has made Edgar
    Winter unique in rock and roll?
    a. he is 6'11", the tallest rocker
    b. he has six fingers on one hand
    c. he is albino

3. Which famous seventies guitarist produced and later
    played for the Edgar Winter Group?
    a. Rick Derringer
    b. Stevie Winwood
    c. Randy Bachman

4. What was the band's only number one hit?
    a. "Easy Street"
    b. "Frankenstein"
    c. "Free Ride"

5. In "Free Ride," what does the Edgar Winter Group say they'll do?
    a. help you see the light
    b. be your lover and your friend
    c. lead you to the Promised Land

Yardbirds

1. Who of the following was *not* a guitarist at one time for the Yardbirds?
    a. Pete Townshend
    b. Eric Clapton
    c. Jimmy Page

2. What was the name of the newly formed group after the Yardbirds broke up, prior to the renaming of the new group as Led Zeppelin?
    a. Heavy Metal Thunder
    b. the New Yardbirds
    c. the Bluesbreakers

3. In "Shapes of Things," the Yardbirds wonder, when tomorrow comes, _____
    a. Will they be bolder than today?
    b. Will you still love them?
    c. What will be the shape of the world?

4. In "Heart Full of Soul," what thought do the Yardbirds echo?
    a. Does anybody really know what time it is?
    b. Where is she?
    c. What is the reason for falling in love?

5. What celestial body would the Yardbirds give "For Your Love"?

a. the sun
b. the world
c. a galaxy

Young Rascals

1. From which early sixties group did three of the original four Young Rascals come?
   a. the Ventures
   b. Joey Dee and the Starliters
   c. the Danleers

2. Although it never broke into the Top Forty charts, what was the Young Rascals' debut single?
   a. "You Better Run"
   b. "I Ain't Gonna Eat Out My Heart Anymore"
   c. "It's Wonderful"

3. In what now historic 1965 concert did the Young Rascals play?
   a. Altamont
   b. the Newport Folk Festival
   c. Shea Stadium

4. What was the band's biggest hit, topping the charts for five weeks?
   a. "People Got to Be Free"
   b. "Good Lovin'"
   c. "Groovin'"

5. How will life be for the Young Rascals as they are "Groovin'" endlessly with you?
   a. unreal
   b. ecstasy
   c. groovy

Frank Zappa

1. Where was Frank Zappa born?

    a. Prague, Czechoslovakia
    b. Dumbarton, Scotland
    c. Baltimore, Maryland

2. What was the name of Frank Zappa's offbeat backup band of the sixties and seventies?
    a. the GTO's
    b. Ruben and the Jets
    c. the Mothers of Invention

3. What well-known duo backed Frank Zappa in his early seventies live appearances?
    a. Marilyn McCoo and Billy Davis Jr.
    b. John and Michelle Phillips
    c. Howard Kaylan and Mark Volman

4. What 1971 movie did Frank Zappa make as a fictionalized "documentary" of his band?
    a. *Uncle Meat*
    b. *Crackers*
    c. *200 Motels*

5. What 1973 hit commemorated a 1971 performance by Zappa at the Montreaux Casino in Switzerland, in which a fire destroyed the building as well as $50,000 in his band's music equipment?
    a. "We're an American Band"
    b. "Dancing in the Moonlight"
    c. "Smoke on the Water"

Zombies

1. From what country did the Zombies' members come?
    a. Australia
    b. the USA
    c. England

2. In what year was the Zombies' last hit, "Time of the Season," recorded?

   a. 1965
   b. 1967
   c. 1969

3. Which member of the Zombies scored a Top Ten solo hit in 1972?
   a. Colin Bluntstone
   b. Chris White
   c. Rod Argent

4. In "She's Not There," how do the Zombies describe the girl's eyes?
   a. clear and bright
   b. green and pretty
   c. weak and bloodshot

5. What do the Zombies say it is time for in "Time of the Season"?
   a. lovin'
   b. movin' on
   c. getting married

ZZ Top

1. Who was the inspiration for the name ZZ Top?
   a. the manager of a professional football team
   b. Texas blues singer Z. Z. Hill
   c. rock star Iggy Pop

2. What underground psychedelic sixties band did ZZ Top leader Billy Gibbons form?
   a. Moby Grape
   b. the Moving Sidewalks
   c. Southwest F.O.B.

3. In what state is ZZ Top revered as a legendary icon?
   a. Arkansas
   b. Texas

    c. Alabama

4. Of the three ZZ Top members, which one doesn't have a long beard?

    a. Billy Gibbons

    b. Dusty Hill

    c. Frank Beard

5. ZZ Top has long been a touring sensation. To ensure their future success, where did the band make an advance booking reservation in 1987 to go to?

    a. the Grammy award ceremonies in the year 2000

    b. Woodstock +50

    c. the moon

II

Across the Charts:
Classic Rock Artist Trivia

1. The Band was the backup for which famous rocker in the sixties?
   a. Bob Dylan
   b. Del Shannon
   c. Elvis Presley

2. From what sixties rock band did two members and the manager of Atlanta Rhythm Section emanate?
   a. the Turtles
   b. Blood, Sweat and Tears
   c. the Classics IV

3. Why was the Kingsmen's biggest hit, "Louie Louie," investigated by the FBI and the FCC?
   a. due to conflict with Paul Revere and the Raiders' version
   b. it failed to list the band's name
   c. because of its reportedly obscene lyrics

4. What was Billy Idol's birth name?
   a. Chad Arthur
   b. Bill Grundy
   c. William Broad

5. What nickname accompanied David Bowie in the seventies?
   a. Crossfire
   b. the Thin White Duke
   c. Major Tom

6. In what two famous music scenes did Santana appear in 1968–69?
   a. Fillmore West and Woodstock
   b. Monterey Pop and San Francisco Park
   c. Altamont and Whiskey A-Go-Go

7. Who had the lead role in the movie *Tommy*?
   a. Elton John

    b. Roger Daltrey

    c. David Bowie

8. In what movie did Survivor's number one hit "Eye of the Tiger" appear?

    a. *An Officer and a Gentleman*

    b. *Rocky III*

    c. *The Karate Kid Part II*

9. For what word is the name Devo a shortened form?

    a. "devour"

    b. "redevelopment"

    c. "de-evolution"

10. Which famous seventies rocker began singing at age fifteen for the McCoys?

    a. Ted Nugent

    b. Rod Argent

    c. Rick Derringer

11. Which of the following pairs are *not* the names of Zappa's children?

    a. Ahmet Rodan and Diva

    b. Bongo and Jawaka

    c. Moon Unit and Dweezil

12. Where was the Left Banke from?

    a. Manchester, England

    b. Sydney, Australia

    c. New York

13. What was Alice Cooper's birth name?

    a. Vincent Furnier

    b. Reginald Dwight

    c. Arnold Wiggins

14. What was Vanilla Fudge's only Top Ten hit?

    a. "You Keep Me Hangin' On"

    b. "Eleanor Rigby"

    c. "Take Me for a Little While"

15. For which of the following did Todd Rundgren *not* produce an album?
    a. Grand Funk Railroad
    b. Aerosmith
    c. Badfinger

16. In what TV soap opera did Rick Springfield have a regular role?
    a. *As the World Turns*
    b. *The Guiding Light*
    c. *General Hospital*

17. Who was Elton John's "Daniel" originally written about?
    a. a Vietnam veteran
    b. Elton John's drummer, Nigel Olsson
    c. Danny Thomas

18. In what 1990 movie did ZZ Top appear?
    a. *Batman*
    b. *Graffiti Bridge*
    c. *Back to the Future III*

19. What heavy-rock garage band did Ted Nugent form in the late sixties?
    a. the Thirteenth Floor Elevators
    b. the Shadows of Knight
    c. the Amboy Dukes

20. What group did Box Tops leader Alex Chilton form in the early seventies?
    a. Alive and Kicking
    b. Big Star
    c. Hotlegs

21. In what year did the rock band Styx form?
    a. 1964
    b. 1970
    c. 1974

22. For which club did Frank Zappa and the Mothers play in 1965?
    a. the Greenwich Village Night Owl
    b. the Whiskey A-Go-Go
    c. Ciro's

23. After what were Dexys Midnight Runners named?
    a. dexedrine, a widely used upper
    b. the manager's pet hamster
    c. an early-forties cowboy movie

24. What group did Outsiders' lead singer Sonny Geraci form in the early seventies?
    a. Atlanta Rhythm Section
    b. Climax
    c. Orleans

25. What Top Five Survivor hit came from the movie *Rocky IV*?
    a. "I Can't Hold Back"
    b. "The Search Is Over"
    c. "Burning Heart"

26. What was Santana's only song not sung in English to break into the Top Twenty charts?
    a. "Oye Como Va"
    b. "Jingo"
    c. "Samba Pa Ti"

27. What name did Alice Cooper use for his band before noticing that it was already the name of a band?
    a. the Kiss
    b. the G.T.O.'s
    c. the Nazz

28. What famous 1969 music festival did Sly and the Family Stone *not* appear at?
    a. Altamont
    b. the Newport Jazz Festival

   c. Woodstock

29. What London-based punk band did Billy Idol lead in the late seventies?
   a. Generation X
   b. Sex Pistols
   c. Roxy Music

30. Why did Kansas change their name from White Clover?
   a. they wanted a name that avoided racial association
   b. another local group was already called White Clover
   c. they were all from Kansas

31. From what group's B-side track did the McCoys derive their name?
   a. the Beatles
   b. the Crystals
   c. the Ventures

32. What accolade did the Cars receive in 1979?
   a. Grammy award for Song of the Year
   b. Elektra Records' "Elektric Rock" award
   c. *Rolling Stone*'s "Best New Band of the Year"

33. Who was Elton John's "Empty Garden" written about?
   a. Marilyn Monroe
   b. John Lennon
   c. John F. Kennedy

34. Todd Rundgren's most successful single was his 1973 release of which song recorded by his band, Nazz, in 1969?
   a. "I Saw the Light"
   b. "Hello It's Me"
   c. "We Gotta Get You a Woman"

35. At what now infamous concert did the Grateful Dead perform in 1969?

    a. Altamont
    b. the Monterey Pop Festival
    c. Golden Gate Park

36. In what city were the Beau Brummels formed?
    a. London
    b. New York City
    c. San Francisco

37. The Allman Brothers Band was the first group to record under a new Atlantic record label. What was the name of the label?
    a. Arista
    b. Capricorn
    c. Chrysalis

38. What is Donovan's last name?
    a. Leitch
    b. Spedding
    c. Sturdley

39. Which of the following groups did the Vanilla Fudge *not* perform with in its 1967 debut at the Village Theatre?
    a. Byrds
    b. Seeds
    c. Outsiders

40. What was Frank Zappa's only Top Forty hit?
    a. "Dancin' Fool"
    b. "Burnt Weeny Sandwich"
    c. "Valley Girl"

41. What recreational activity is Ted Nugent well-known for?
    a. hunting
    b. hang gliding
    c. mountain climbing

42. From what country did Blue Öyster Cult originate?

    a. Denmark
    b. Germany
    c. the USA

43. Styx was originally known as TW4. Why did they use this abbreviation rather than the name the initials stood for?

    a. to avoid confusion with the group the Trade Winds
    b. to satisfy angry Trans World Airlines lawyers
    c. to capitalize on the British success of the DC5

44. What Top Five hit was sung by a member of Survivor in an earlier band in 1970?

    a. "All Right Now"/Free
    b. "Ride Captain Ride"/Blues Image
    c. "Vehicle"/Ides of March

45. What was Billy Idol's only number one hit in the U.S.?

    a. "Mony Mony"
    b. "Rebel Yell"
    c. "Eyes Without a Face"

46. Which album by the Band featured several Dylan tracks and has become one of rock's classics?

    a. *The Wall*
    b. *Music From Big Pink*
    c. *Great White Wonder*

47. What was the actual incident that later inspired Elton John's "Someone Saved My Life Tonight"?

    a. a reunion between Elton John and Bernie Taupin
    b. the winning of three Grammy awards
    c. a suicide attempt by Elton John

48. Which organization selected Kansas as the first group to represent them as its Deputy Ambassadors of Goodwill?

    a. UNICEF

    b. the Boy Scouts of America

    c. the Benevolent Protective Order of Elks

49. In which 1970 music festival did the Allman Brothers Band play alongside Jimi Hendrix, among others?

    a. Fillmore East

    b. Woodstock

    c. the Atlanta International Pop Festival

50. What well-known British group backed Donovan in his *Barabajagal* album?

    a. the Jeff Beck Group

    b. the Moody Blues

    c. the Hollies

III

De Doo Doo Doo, De Da Da Da: Classic Rock Lyrics Questions

Easy as A-B-C
LEVEL ONE

1. In Simon and Garfunkel's "The Sounds of Silence," what are the streets paved with?
   a. cobblestone
   b. gold
   c. rolling stones

2. How do the Youngbloods define love in "Get Together"?
   a. it's worth all the gold on earth
   b. it's a song
   c. it's how we feel for one another

3. While "The Cisco Kid" drank whiskey, what does War say Pancho drank?
   a. wine
   b. water
   c. tequila

4. In "Wooly Bully," what do Sam the Sham and the Pharaohs ask us to learn to do?
   a. treat animals with respect
   b. dance
   c. say "please"

5. What kind of car did Jan and Dean race against in "Dead Man's Curve"?
   a. a Jaguar
   b. a Volkswagen
   c. a Porsche

6. In "Lay Lady Lay," what is Bob Dylan's bed made of?
   a. wood

    b. nails

    c. brass

7. According to Peter, Paul and Mary in "I Dig Rock & Roll Music," which group has got a good thing going as long as their words don't get in the way?

    a. the Beatles

    b. the Mamas and the Papas

    c. Frank Zappa and the Mothers of Invention

8. Because "You Can Do Magic," what does America say you can have?

    a. the world at your command

    b. ten thousand faithful followers

    c. anything you desire

9. In "Take It Easy," which city and state are the Eagles in when they espy a girl driving by them?

    a. Houston, Texas

    b. Kansas City, Missouri

    c. Winslow, Arizona

10. In "Who'll Stop the Rain," what does Creedence Clearwater Revival say is on the ground?

    a. hungry hearts

    b. confusion

    c. people drowning in their tears

11. While they're "Truckin'," what does the Grateful Dead say lately has occurred to them?

    a. that they're riding on an empty tank

    b. that there's no one on the roads anymore

    c. what a long strange trip it's been

12. What does John Lennon say it isn't hard to "Imagine"?

    a. that times will soon be better

    b. that there's no country

    c. that love is the word

13. In "Baby Hold on," what does Eddie Money say about the future?

    a. it's his and yours to see
    b. it'll be worth waiting for
    c. no one can stop it from coming

14. In "Hang On Sloopy," what does everybody try to do to the McCoys' girl?
    a. tug on her buckteeth
    b. steal her away from them
    c. put her down

15. In "California Dreamin'," what color are the skies, according to the Mamas and the Papas?
    a. gray
    b. clear
    c. sunny

16. In "I've Been Lonely Too Long," what do the Young Rascals feel they can't go on anymore without?
    a. love
    b. friends
    c. dreams

17. According to Crosby, Stills and Nash, toward what famous city would you take the "Marrakesh Express" southbound to reach Marrakesh?
    a. Berlin
    b. Casablanca
    c. Woodstock

18. Why do the Zombies advise the other boy to "Tell Her No" even if she tempts him with her charms?
    a. she's a tease
    b. her love belongs to them
    c. because then he'll have her under his thumb

19. While going to "Surf City," what do Jan and Dean say they'll do if their car breaks down along the way?
    a. they'll tow it all the way there
    b. they'll catch a cab

    c. they'll hitch a ride

20. What did the Boxtops' girlfriend say to them in "The Letter"?

    a. to leave her alone

    b. that she couldn't live without them

    c. that she's coming home

21. According to Barry McGuire in "Eve of Destruction," what part of the world is exploding in wars?

    a. the northern hemisphere

    b. all parts

    c. the Eastern world

22. How does Tommy Roe feel when he goes for a ride with "Sheila"?

    a. like a pimp

    b. like a king

    c. funny inside

23. In "C'mon Let's Go," what does Ritchie Valens want his girlfriend to tell him she'll never do?

    a. get angry with him

    b. leave him

    c. make him jealous

24. In Elvis Presley's "Jailhouse Rock," who was playing the saxophone?

    a. Spider Murphy

    b. Jim Dandy

    c. Leroy Brown

25. In "Like a Rolling Stone," because nobody's ever taught you how to live out on the street, what does Bob Dylan say you're going to have to do?

    a. get used to it

    b. learn how to fend for yourself

    c. join the welfare lines

26. Although "Silence Is Golden," what can't the Tremeloes ignore?

    a. that their eyes still see
    b. the writing on the wall
    c. the pounding of their heart

27. In "Bend Me, Shape Me," what three things can you turn the American Breed from a beggar into?
    a. a lover, husband, or father
    b. a king, clown, or poet
    c. a lion, tiger, or bear

28. In "Walk Away Renee," although the Left Banke says the sidewalks are not the same, what do they add?
    a. it's such a shame
    b. you're not to blame
    c. they're still insane

29. According to the Rolling Stones' "Ruby Tuesday," what will happen if you lose your dreams?
    a. she'll find them for you
    b. you'll finally wake up
    c. you'll lose your mind

30. Because Eddie Cochran has a bad case of the "Summertime Blues," how long does he want to take off from work to go on a vacation?
    a. the entire summer
    b. two months
    c. two weeks

31. What does Creedence Clearwater Revival ask you to bring along as you go "Up Around the Bend"?
    a. your suitcase and belongings
    b. your hopes and wishes
    c. a song and a smile

32. In "I Need Your Love Tonight," what does Elvis Presley have on high?
    a. his lovin'
    b. his hi-fi

c. his hopes

33. What is it that the Beatles say they don't care too much for because it "Can't Buy Me Love"?

    a. fancy clothes

    b. foolish promises

    c. money

34. According to Peter, Paul and Mary in "Don't Think Twice (It's Alright)," when will they be gone?

    a. when the rooster crows

    b. when you tell them to go

    c. in a million years

35. Where does the J. Geils Band see their "Centerfold"?

    a. in their dreams

    b. in a girlie magazine

    c. by the record machine

36. In "I Want You to Want Me," what is Cheap Trick begging you to do?

    a. beg them

    b. say you will

    c. dance with them

37. In "She's Just My Style," what is it about her that drives Gary Lewis and the Playboys wild?

    a. her friends

    b. her name

    c. the way she moves

38. In Stephen Stills's "Love the One You're With," who does the eagle fly with?

    a. the falconer's glove

    b. the dove

    c. your love

39. In "Rain on the Roof," what are the Lovin' Spoonful caught up in?

    a. a summer shower

    b. lies

    c. love

40. How many ships are served daily in the port in which Looking Glass's "Brandy" works?

    a. a thousand

    b. twenty

    c. a hundred

41. Santana cautions that you'd better change your "Evil Ways" before they start to do what?

    a. move in with you

    b. love you

    c. leave you

42. In "Jack and Diane," what does John Cougar say you try to hold on to as long as you can?

    a. your dreams

    b. sixteen

    c. your parents

43. In "Crazy Little Thing Called Love," what does Queen say their girl gives them?

    a. headaches and pain

    b. a reason to wake up each day

    c. hot and cold fever

44. What do the Classics IV want "Stormy" to bring back?

    a. their money

    b. that sunny day

    c. their baby

45. In "A Horse With No Name," how long did America let their horse run free because the desert had turned to sea?

    a. three days

    b. nine days

    c. six weeks

46. In "My Ding-a-Ling," what does Chuck Berry say those who won't sing must be doing?

    a. playing hard to get

    b. sleeping

    c. playing with their own ding-a-ling

47. What does Carl Perkins have in his "Matchbox"?

    a. matches

    b. old photographs

    c. his clothes

48. Now that the Boxtops have lost their girlfriend and "Cry Like a Baby," what has every road become?

    a. a lonely street

    b. a busy freeway

    c. a dead-end driveway

49. In "Sara," what does Starship say no time is a good time for?

    a. fussing and fighting

    b. bringing up the past to feed a hungry heart

    c. saying goodbye

50. In "I'm a Man," what can't Chicago help but do?

    a. carry an attitude

    b. love you so

    c. all they can

51. According to Loggins and Messina in "Your Mama Don't Dance," what time do the old folks want you to be home by after a night of entertaining?

    a. midnight

    b. dawn

    c. 10:00 P.M.

52. In "I Love Rock 'N Roll," where did Joan Jett see him dancing?

    a. in the middle of the dance floor

    b. by the record machine

    c. up on the stage

53. What are the Kinks doing on a "Sunny Afternoon"?

   a. thinkin'
   b. makin' love to you
   c. lazin'

54. According to the Buggles in "Video Killed the Radio Star," why can't we rewind?
   a. because life has already passed us by
   b. because we've gone too far
   c. because the bullets are still in the radio

55. What does Gary U.S. Bonds plan to do until "Quarter to Three"?
   a. drink
   b. dance
   c. make love to you

56. Who does Dion's "Donna, the Prima Donna" want to be like?
   a. the Mona Lisa
   b. Madonna
   c. Zsa Zsa Gabor

57. According to the Band in "The Night They Drove Old Dixie Down," what can't you do to a Caine when he's in his grave in defeat?
   a. raise him back up
   b. push him any lower
   c. make him pay you back

58. In "Suite Judy Blue Eyes," what days do Crosby, Stills and Nash want you to come see them?
   a. Tuesdays and Thursdays
   b. Thursdays and Saturdays
   c. Fridays and Saturdays

59. In "Proud Mary," what city does Creedence Clearwater Revival say doesn't compare to rolling down the river in their riverboat queen?
   a. New Orleans

    b. Baton Rouge

    c. Dallas

60. How much "Real Love" do the Doobie Brothers want?

    a. one minute

    b. as much as time allows

    c. twenty-four hours a day

61. According to the Grateful Dead, "Casey Jones" is high on _____.

    a. life

    b. his own horse

    c. cocaine

62. In "Blinded by the Light," what did the little early-birdie ask Manfred Mann's Earth Band?

    a. if they wanted to share a meal

    b. if they needed a ride

    c. why they were sleeping so late

63. When the Monkees say to take the "Last Train to Clarksville," where do they plan to meet you?

    a. at the station

    b. at their house

    c. on the train

64. In "God Only Knows," what do the Beach Boys say would happen if you should ever leave them?

    a. life would still go on

    b. they would go crazy

    c. they would vow to never get married

65. In "Give a Little Bit," what does Supertramp say you have to do and then you'll be surprised?

    a. take the hand of the man with the lonely eyes

    b. drop the rumors and the lies and live a life free from disguise

    c. quit your job and say goodbye, then sail away for paradise

66. What does ZZ Top say about her "Legs"?
- **a.** they're really skinny
- **b.** she knows how to use them
- **c.** it's the only part of her they see

67. In "My Generation," what does the Who ask the older generation to do?
- **a.** fade away
- **b.** get with it
- **c.** dance to the beat

68. What does "Peg" do that makes Steely Dan love them better?
- **a.** she smiles for the camera
- **b.** she puts Al in his place
- **c.** she whispers sweet words in the dark

69. In "I'm On Fire," how does Bruce Springsteen compare the feeling he has?
- **a.** it's like someone's made a six-inch knife cut through the middle of his soul
- **b.** it's a passion that only love can tame
- **c.** he's a fever that has only one cure, and you're the doctor with the motion potion

70. According to Elton John in "Bennie and the Jets," what did he see in the magazine that she had?
- **a.** electric boots and a mohair suit
- **b.** groupies and fan clubs
- **c.** hair flowing like angel wings

71. After what happens does Fleetwood Mac say you'll see your "Gypsy"?
- **a.** you close your eyes and dream
- **b.** the lights go out
- **c.** lightning strikes

72. Who did Jimi Hendrix's "Hey Joe" shoot?
- **a.** his woman's secret lover

    b. his old lady

    c. himself

73. America is singing for all the "Lonely People" who think _____.

    a. we're on the road to ruin

    b. love has passed them by

    c. life is worth living proud and free

74. In "We're an American Band," how long does Grand Funk say they were out on the road?

    a. six long nights

    b. longer than they could bear

    c. forty days

75. What do the Eagles say you can't do with your "Lyin' Eyes"?

    a. escape from the truth

    b. keep them from seeing

    c. hide

76. In "Rainy Day Women #12 & 35," what does Bob Dylan say everybody should do?

    a. love one another

    b. get out of the rain

    c. get stoned

77. Because "School's Out," what does Alice Cooper say we won't have any more of?

    a. friends to see or things to do

    b. education through indoctrination

    c. pencils, books, and teachers' dirty looks

78. What kind of hair is it that makes the Barbarians wonder "Are You a Boy or Are You a Girl"?

    a. hair tied in a ponytail

    b. long blond hair

    c. dreadlocks

79. In "Drive," what do the Cars say you can't go on thinking?

    a. nothing's wrong
    b. living is free
    c. that they love someone else

80. According to A Flock of Seagulls in "I Ran (So Far Away)," what appears above your head?
    a. a cloud
    b. a flock of seagulls
    c. stars

81. In "We Belong," what does Pat Benatar want to do?
    a. leave you
    b. make you forgive her
    c. be friends with you

82. What does Pete Townshend want you to "Let My Love Open the Door" to?
    a. the street
    b. your heart
    c. paradise

83. According to Greg Kihn Band, what is in "Jeopardy"?
    a. the freedom to say what you want
    b. the future of the whole human race
    c. their love

84. On the "Highway to Hell," where does AC/DC say they're going?
    a. to the Promised Land
    b. to a weekend dance
    c. to your mother's house

85. In "Owner of a Lonely Heart," what does Yes say you always live your life without doing?
    a. talking it over with them
    b. giving everyone else an even break
    c. thinking of the future

86. What is it that the Reflections must find tomorrow to avoid having their love be destroyed by a tragedy "Just Like Romeo and Juliet"?

   a. work
   b. a girl to call their own
   c. the way to your heart

87. What is the name of the girl Rod Stewart asks to "Stay With Me"?

   a. Rita
   b. Sue
   c. Maggie

88. In "Eyes Without a Face," what does Billy Idol tell you to do when he's far from home?

   a. stay soft and pure
   b. think of him once in a while
   c. don't call him

89. Where does Dion, the "Lonely Teenager," want to go?

   a. to school
   b. home
   c. into your heart

90. What kind of athlete do Jan and Dean say you are when you go "Sidewalk Surfin'"?

   a. a daring athlete
   b. a pathetic athlete
   c. an asphalt athlete

91. According to Elton John, what time is "zero-hour" for the "Rocket Man"?

   a. 12:00 midnight
   b. 4:00 P.M.
   c. 9:00 A.M.

92. What do the Grass Roots want "Temptation Eyes" to do tonight?

   a. stop their crying
   b. look their way
   c. love them

93. In "Born to Be Wild," what does Steppenwolf say you should look for when you get your motor running and head out on the highway?

   a. cops
   b. adventure
   c. a wild-eyed honey

94. From what city are Canned Heat "Going Up the Country"?

   a. New Orleans
   b. Detroit
   c. Los Angeles

95. In "You Were on My Mind," why did We Five go to the corner?

   a. to watch the cars go by
   b. to ease their pain
   c. to telephone you

96. What's going to happen tomorrow morning to Chuck Berry's "Sweet Little Sixteen"?

   a. she's going to be yelled at by her mom
   b. she'll be back in school
   c. she'll find a new boyfriend

97. In "Long Cool Woman," when the Hollies were working downtown, what did they have by their side?

   a. their woman
   b. a whiskey bottle
   c. a gun

98. In "Addicted to Love," what does Robert Palmer say about you even though the lights are on?

   a. you're not home
   b. you're as cold as ice
   c. the thrill is gone

99. Where does Todd Rundgren say "I Saw the Light"?

   a. in your eyes

    b. in the night

    c. at the end of the tunnel

100. In "Eye of the Tiger," now that Survivor has done their time, what do they call themselves?

    a. just another loser

    b. just a man and his will to survive

    c. slave to no man

Two Out of Three Ain't Bad
LEVEL TWO

1. According to Devo in "Whip It," what should you break?
   a. your bad habits
   b. your mama's back
   c. their spirit

2. In "Hit Me With Your Best Shot," Pat Benatar calls you _____.
   a. a loaded pistol
   b. a tough cookie
   c. a freaked-out commie

3. According to Ambrosia, "You're the Only Woman" that they've been _____.
   a. trying to avoid
   b. true to
   c. dreaming of

4. What does Rick Springfield wish about "Jessie's Girl"?
   a. that he could be in her shoes
   b. that he could have her
   c. that she'd leave him alone

5. According to Styx, what part of "Mr. Roboto" is made by IBM?
   a. his body
   b. his brain
   c. his heart

6. In "I Just Want to Celebrate," what did Rare Earth get their hands on, though it blew away?
   a. a dollar bill

    b. a dream

    c. the key to your heart

7. What do the Rolling Stones say they'll do one day with their "Wild Horses"?

    a. ride them

    b. shoot all of them

    c. set them all free

8. According to Patti Smith, what can't others do "Because the Night" belongs to lovers?

    a. tell you how to live your life

    b. make you lose your dreams

    c. hurt you

9. Elvis Presley doesn't want the "Little Sister" to kiss him once or twice and then _____.

    a. tell her parents

    b. run

    c. say goodnight

10. Because "There's Got to Be a Word" that means more than love, who do the Innocence say could probably find such a word?

    a. Romeo and Juliet

    b. Mr. Webster

    c. you and them

11. In "Time Won't Let Me," what have the Outsiders waited too long for?

    a. a chance to hold you in their arms

    b. happiness to come into their life

    c. for you to say goodbye to your other boyfriend

12. In "Blowin' in the Wind," Peter, Paul and Mary question how many times cannonballs must fly before _____.

    a. they're forever banned

    b. the world is destroyed

   c. we reach peace

13. At what hour are the Soul Survivors caught in the traffic jam upon the "Expressway to Your Heart"?

   a. 8:00 A.M.

   b. noon

   c. 5:00 P.M.

14. What does Sugarloaf call their "Green-Eyed Lady"?

   a. the apple of their eye

   b. a child of nature and friend of man

   c. virtue and beauty in an angel's face

15. As they are "Homeward Bound," where are Simon and Garfunkel sitting?

   a. in a Greyhound bus

   b. in a railroad station

   c. on a Boeing 747

16. In "I Fought the Law," why did the Bobby Fuller Four steal money?

   a. because someone dared them to

   b. because they had none

   c. they didn't—they were wrongly accused

17. For Jay and the Americans, "This Magic Moment" is sweeter than wine and softer than _____.

   a. a summer's night

   b. a pillow

   c. a quiet cloud

18. What do the Beach Boys say happens when you "Catch a Wave"?

   a. you lose sight of tomorrow

   b. you can't be beat

   c. you're sitting on top of the world

19. In "Can't You Hear My Heart Beat," what is the explanation Herman's Hermits give for their unusual palpitations?

    a. you're the one they love

    b. they know the time to win your heart is near

    c. you're the doctor and you've got the cure

20. In "A Groovy Kind of Love," when the Mindbenders are feeling blue, what do they do to remedy the feeling?

    a. take a look at you

    b. say a prayer for a love so true and dream of you

    c. turn on their favorite radio station

21. In "The Twist," where is Chubby Checker's daddy?

    a. sleeping

    b. shopping

    c. working

22. Who told the Four Seasons to give up their girlfriend and "Walk Like a Man"?

    a. their friends

    b. the camp counselor

    c. their father

23. In "Turn! Turn! Turn!" the Byrds say there's a time to dance, a time to _____.

    a. gather dreams

    b. mourn

    c. make romance

24. In "Hey Baby (They're Playing Our Song)," what kind of melody does the Buckinghams' special song have?

    a. a melody of love

    b. enchanting

    c. pretty

25. In "New Kid in Town," what do the Eagles say about how your old friends treat you?

    a. they treat you just fine

    b. they don't even remember your name

    c. they treat you like you're something new

26. In "Don't Bring Me Down," what does Electric Light Orchestra say you want to do?

    a. go out with your fancy friends

    b. get married

    c. make them feel that they're the guilty ones

27. Where has Heart decided to head "Straight On"?

    a. to paradise

    b. to Memphis

    c. for you

28. In "Kiss on My List," Daryl Hall and John Oates say that your kiss is on what specific list?

    a. the list of the ten best reasons for falling in love

    b. the list of things that will never come true

    c. the list of the best things in life

29. The Lovin' Spoonful are lost in their "Daydream" about what?

    a. their bundle of joy

    b. a delicious barbecue steak dinner

    c. the party Friday night

30. In "Tuesday Afternoon," what are drawing the Moody Blues near?

    a. your words of love

    b. the sounds of silence

    c. the trees

31. What does the Steve Miller Band say is one thing people call "The Joker"?

    a. the gangster of love

    b. a poet of life

    c. a lover of fools

32. In "Double Vision," what does Foreigner say they're going to push it to the limit by doing?

    a. living all their years in a single minute

    b. enjoying both the good times and the bad times in it

    c. fighting for your love until they win it

33. In "Lady Willpower," what do Gary Puckett and the Union Gap tell their girlfriend that it's now or never to do?
    a. get married
    b. give her love to them
    c. decide if love will last

34. In "Another One Bites the Dust," what does Queen say you did for them?
    a. you helped them make it through thick and thin
    b. you took them for everything they had
    c. you gave them hope and inspiration

35. As they "Ramble On," what does Led Zeppelin say it's time to do?
    a. pay up their dues or face the blues
    b. sing their song
    c. hitch a ride to another town

36. According to Styx, what is true between them and "Babe"?
    a. they're not trying to tie her down
    b. they love her
    c. they hit more home runs in a single season

37. What's in the garage of Jan and Dean's "Little Old Lady From Pasadena"?
    a. a stolen Mustang
    b. cans of paint and gasoline
    c. a super-stock Dodge

38. In "Love Is All Around," what do the Troggs say you gave to them and they gave to you?
    a. a disease
    b. a promise
    c. a ring

39. In "Sloop John B," what were the Beach Boys doing all night that caused them to get into a fight?
    a. gambling

    b. talking to their girl

    c. drinking

40. In "American Pie," what touched Don McLean deep inside?

    a. the day the music died

    b. a knife with a six-inch blade

    c. the sound of your voice

41. According to Wayne Fontana and the Mindbenders in "Game of Love," what did Adam say to Eve in the Garden of Eden?

    a. baby, you're for me

    b. there's no time like the right time, and the right time is now

    c. you're the apple of my eye

42. In "Sweet Home Alabama," what does Lynyrd Skynyrd say about their Southern man?

    a. he doesn't need Neil Young around

    b. he's the luckiest man in the world

    c. he's got the sweetest Southern belle

43. What question does Dion ask of "Ruby Baby"?

    a. When will she be his?

    b. When is she coming home?

    c. Does she love him?

44. While searching for his "Heart of Gold," what city does Neil Young mention he's been to?

    a. Hollywood

    b. Tampa

    c. Dallas

45. What do the Animals say moves on warm "San Franciscan Nights"?

    a. cars and trucks

    b. walls and minds

    c. lots of drugs

46. In "Hushabye," who do the Mystics say will be coming soon to sing you a slumber tune?
   a. the sandman
   b. Freddy
   c. Cupid

47. In "Never My Love," what does the Association say you are afraid they might one day do?
   a. cheat on you
   b. change their mind
   c. go all the way

48. What do the Four Seasons want to do all night with "Sherry"?
   a. walk along the beach
   b. dance
   c. count the stars in the sky

49. In "It's Up to You," what would Ricky Nelson give up everything he owns for?
   a. a chance to be a teen idol again
   b. the chance to have you near
   c. the chance to pound your other boyfriend

50. In "Hello, Hello," the Sopwith Camel knows that they'll never treat you _____.
   a. differently
   b. nice
   c. mean

51. In "Please Please Me," what do the Beatles say you don't need them to do?
   a. give you money
   b. show you the way
   c. dress in drag

52. What two things did Chuck Berry miss until he was "Back in the U.S.A."?
   a. skyscrapers and freeways

   b. sunshine and girls
   c. taxi cabs and all-night clubs

53. What did the "Heat of the Moment" tell Asia?
   a. what their heart meant
   b. that love is really hot
   c. that nothing lasts forever

54. In "Cuts Like a Knife," although Bryan Adams took it all for granted, what didn't he know?
   a. that you'd be letting him go
   b. that words can cut both ways
   c. that you weren't just another meal

55. In "Rock and Roll Hoochie Koo," what is Rick Derringer doing that he hopes you're all doing, too?
   a. dancing to the beat
   b. living your dreams
   c. getting high all the time

56. What did a girl do to put Jimi Hendrix in a cloud of "Purple Haze"?
   a. she put a spell on him
   b. she asked him out on a date
   c. she said she loved him

57. What do the Animals want to do as long as you "Don't Bring Me Down"?
   a. be your only boyfriend
   b. provide for you
   c. make you feel high

58. In "Imaginary Lover," what does Atlanta Rhythm Section say is their private pleasure?
   a. a midnight fantasy
   b. talking with you on the telephone
   c. listening to the oldies at night

59. In "How Can I Be Sure," what are the Rascals unsure about?

    a. your love for them
    b. whether they'll be sure with you
    c. whether there's a test tomorrow

60. What do the Small Faces say they'll do at "Itchycoo Park"?
    a. fall in love
    b. get high
    c. watch the children play

61. As they spend "Saturday in the Park," what does Chicago say people are doing there?
    a. playing baseball
    b. walking in the dark
    c. dancing and laughing

62. What do the Cars say "You Might Think" because they hang around with you?
    a. that they really like you a lot
    b. that they're crazy
    c. that they have no place else to go

63. In "Pleasant Valley Sunday," who do the Monkees say is so serene because he has a television in every room?
    a. Mr. Green
    b. Mr. Jones
    c. Mr. Bruhn

64. In "The Long Run," what did the Eagles used to do?
    a. take your love for granted
    b. build up paper dreams in the middle of a storm
    c. hurry a lot

65. What happens as the girl leaves the Hollies "On a Carousel"?
    a. she flashes her big brown eyes their way
    b. she drops the present she won before
    c. she meets her boyfriend

66. The Dave Clark Five are "Glad All Over" about what?
   a. that you're theirs
   b. that you're coming home
   c. that their concert tour is almost over

67. In "Just a Little," love has been sweet for the Beau Brummels though it has also been _____.
   a. hard to beat
   b. incomplete
   c. filled with deceit

68. In "Don't Stand So Close to Me," what do the Police say that sometimes it's not so easy to be?
   a. new in town
   b. a hard-nosed guy
   c. the teacher's pet

69. According to Paul Revere and the Raiders, what aren't "Kicks" bringing you?
   a. any answers
   b. peace of mind
   c. happiness

70. What does Santana say the "Black Magic Woman" is trying to do to them?
   a. help them get back with their lady
   b. put a spell of love over them
   c. make a devil out of them

71. What unusual facial feature does Sheb Wooley's "Purple People Eater" possess?
   a. one long horn
   b. a purple hump
   c. a face like Elvis

72. Because it's party time in "FM (No Static at All)," what does Steely Dan want you to do?
   a. turn on the radio
   b. go out and buy some pretzels and beer

    c. kick off your high-heel sneakers

73. In "Fire," what is it that Jimi Hendrix only wants to do?

    a. itch a desire
    b. burn for you
    c. find a way to go higher

74. According to Three Dog Night, where is "An Old-Fashioned Love Song" playing?

    a. on the radio
    b. in their mind
    c. in lovers' hearts

75. Where do the Turtles want to go with "Elenore"?

    a. to a movie
    b. to a party
    c. to the beach

76. Big Brother and the Holding Company say you can take another "Piece of My Heart" if _____.

    a. one piece isn't enough
    b. you want to see their heart break
    c. it makes you feel good

77. In "I'm Looking Through You," what do the Beatles say has a nasty habit of disappearing overnight?

    a. love
    b. faith in believing
    c. their money

78. In "Blue Suede Shoes," from what does Carl Perkins say it's OK to drink his liquor?

    a. his blue suede shoes
    b. an old fruit jar
    c. the bottle

79. What couldn't all the people prevent the Who's "Happy Jack" from being?

    a. abnormal

    b. free

    c. happy

80. In "Space Oddity," what does David Bowie say that ground control wants him to do?

    a. float through the air with the greatest of ease

    b. take his protein pills and put his helmet on

    c. return the ship

81. What question haunts Roy Orbison and has him "Running Scared"?

    a. Is he after you or after me?

    b. Is he related to Charles Manson?

    c. If he came back, which one would you choose?

82. In "All Shook Up," what is Elvis Presley itching like?

    a. a person who's been stung by a bee

    b. a man on a fuzzy tree

    c. a dog trying to find a flea

83. According to Sam the Sham and the Pharaohs, what feature on "Li'l Red Riding Hood" can drive wolves mad?

    a. her eyes

    b. her ruby lips

    c. her shapely hips

84. In "Go Your Own Way," if they could, what would Fleetwood Mac give you?

    a. a swift kick and a slap

    b. a chance to break free

    c. their world

85. Randy and the Rainbows' "Denise" has what color eyes?

    a. rainbow

    b. blue

    c. hazel

86. What does Iron Butterfly want you to know "In-A-Gadda-Da-Vida"?

   a. that they love you
   b. that they can't speak English
   c. that happiness can be found in the forests of your mind

87. In "I Got You Babe," how do Sonny and Cher feel when Cher puts her little hand in Sonny's?
   a. like two grains of sand on the shores of life
   b. kind of funny inside
   c. that there's no mountain they can't climb

88. According to the Beach Boys, what is she wearing that has them picking up "Good Vibrations"?
   a. metallic braces
   b. colorful clothes
   c. a magic smile

89. In "Lightnin' Strikes," what does Lou Christie see waiting for him and his girlfriend?
   a. a chapel
   b. a future of happiness
   c. a shotgun

90. In "You Better You Bet," although the Who has got your body on their mind, what do they return to?
   a. their own work
   b. a house and wife and family
   c. the sound of T. Rex

91. What do the Cyrkle compare with a "Red Rubber Ball"?
   a. the ocean
   b. happy faces
   c. the sun

92. Because she defends them so they don't ever have to speak, what kind of dream does the Band say it is being "Up on Cripple Creek"?
   a. a dream of paralyzing perfection

    b. a drunkard's dream

    c. a lawyer's nightmare

93. In "Different Drum," what are the Stone Poneys not in the market for?

    a. a boy who wants to love only them

    b. a new band

    c. a playboy

94. According to the Rivieras in "California Sun," how are the girls in San Francisco?

    a. frisky

    b. scarce

    c. bitchin'

95. In "Bottle of Wine," how do the Fireballs' pants look?

    a. so old they shine

    b. dirty and ragged

    c. like they've been worn for a year

96. What does Eric Clapton say you should do to "Let It Grow"?

    a. plant your love

    b. shut your mouth

    c. stop shopping so much

97. In "Laugh, Laugh," what do the Beau Brummels say about school?

    a. you don't learn everything there

    b. it's not the only place to pick up chicks

    c. what you learn today, you forget tomorrow

98. How was "Delta Lady" the many times Joe Cocker found her in the garden?

    a. fine and nice

    b. filled with mystery and romance

    c. wet and naked

99. In "There Is a Mountain," whose name does Donovan call?

  a. Juanita
  b. Jennifer
  c. Mama

100. How is the weather where Del Shannon is walking and thinking about his "Runaway"?

  a. sunny
  b. rainy
  c. snowing

Help!

LEVEL THREE

1. How often do the Swingin' Medallions get their "Double Shot"?
   a. twice a day
   b. whenever they pass a bar
   c. once a week

2. According to Billy J. Kramer and the Dakotas in "Bad to Me," why won't you leave them?
   a. because you've got free room and board
   b. because you love them
   c. because you told them so

3. In "Whole Lot of Shakin' Goin' On," what does Jerry Lee Lewis say they have by the horn?
   a. a trumpet
   b. a megaphone
   c. the bull

4. In "Hello, I Love You," what do the Doors want you to do?
   a. lead them to your heart
   b. give love a change
   c. tell them your name

5. In "The Weight," what place did the Band pull into?
   a. Nazareth
   b. Lodi
   c. St. Louis

6. In "When I Was Young" the Animals say that they were so much _____.

    a. wiser
    b. taller
    c. older

7. During his "School Day," who won't leave Chuck Berry alone?
    a. the school bully
    b. the guy behind him
    c. his girlfriend

8. Although the Rivingtons admit that "Papa-Oom-Mow-Mow" is the funniest sound they've ever heard, what do they also admit?
    a. they can't understand a single word
    b. the beat isn't really so absurd
    c. it makes them flutter like a little bird

9. In "Hell Is for Children," how does Pat Benatar say kids shouldn't have to pay for their love?
    a. with their bones and flesh
    b. with promises that can't come true
    c. with money out of their own pockets

10. Though they want to make a secret rendezvous with you because they're "Hot Blooded," what does Foreigner say you've got to do first?
    a. get away from you-know-who
    b. make them even hotter
    c. change into your skin-tight dress and pink high heels

11. How much money does Gregg Allman, the "Midnight Rider," have left?
    a. one dollar
    b. twenty dollars
    c. forty cents

12. In "Takin' Care of Business," what does Bachman-Turner Overdrive advise you to get if you want the chance of going far?

    a. a psychedelic car
    b. a rough and rowdy bar
    c. a secondhand guitar

13. Because they've got their "Private Eyes" on you, what do Daryl Hall and John Oates say they'll know soon enough?
    a. if you've got cheating on your mind
    b. if love is blind or just a hopeless state of mind
    c. whether you're letting them in or letting them go

14. In "We're an American Band," as long as they can make it to the show tonight, what does Grand Funk say will keep them right?
    a. the sounds
    b. the booze and ladies
    c. rhythm and soul

15. In "Sweet Emotion," what did Aerosmith pull into town inside of?
    a. a limousine
    b. a low rider
    c. a police car

16. In "Sara," what does Starship say they'll never do?
    a. find another girl like you
    b. learn how to fly
    c. let their love for you slip away

17. In "Eye of the Tiger," what does Survivor say you must fight just to keep alive?
    a. rumors and lies
    b. the traffic
    c. dreams of the past

18. How old was Ted Nugent when he first got "Cat Scratch Fever"?
    a. ten
    b. seventeen

    c. six months

19. What is the "Wild Night" doing to Van Morrison?

    a. keeping him from sleeping

    b. calling

    c. driving him crazy

20. In "Another Brick in the Wall," what does Pink Floyd say we don't need?

    a. another hero

    b. education

    c. more excuses

21. Where on "Mainstreet" was Bob Seger standing, trying to get his courage up?

    a. on the corner

    b. in the gutter

    c. near the bar

22. What doesn't Van Halen want "Oh, Pretty Woman" to do?

    a. walk on by

    b. tell a silly joke

    c. get married to anyone else

23. Why do Frank Zappa and the Mothers of Invention say "Don't Eat the Yellow Snow"?

    a. it may contain radioactive fallout

    b. because lemons don't fall in the winter

    c. because of the dogs

24. In "Sister Golden Hair," what is America not ready for?

    a. the altar

    b. her constant complaints

    c. everyone else's laughter

25. At approximately what time do Creedence Clearwater say that the kids are starting to assemble "Down on the Corner"?

    a. noon

    b. suppertime

    c. midnight

26. Who did the Doobie Brothers see down the track in "Long Train Runnin'" mourning the loss of her home and family?

    a. their mama

    b. Miss Lucy

    c. Mrs. Jones

27. In "Light My Fire," what do the Doors claim their love could become?

    a. a funeral pyre

    b. a raging inferno

    c. an everlasting monument

28. According to Bob Dylan in "Subterranean Homesick Blues," what don't you need a weatherman to tell you?

    a. whether you're a good writer

    b. how strong your love will be tomorrow

    c. which way the wind blows

29. Fleetwood Mac asks "Rhiannon (Will You Ever Win)" whether you'd stay if she promised you _____.

    a. money

    b. true love

    c. heaven

30. Because they're a "Dirty White Boy," what does Foreigner wonder about them seeing you?

    a. Will it rub off on you?

    b. Will it ruin your reputation?

    c. Will you want to see them again?

31. In "Modern Love," how does the idea of going to the church on time make David Bowie feel?

    a. wonderful

    b. terrified

    c. rushed

32. In "The Air That I Breathe," if the Hollies could make a wish, what would they do?
    a. let their heart lead the way
    b. stop smoking
    c. pass

33. What do the Kingsmen tell "Louie, Louie" that they must do?
    a. tell their parents they're spending the night studying
    b. go home
    c. slip away into the night

34. According to Kansas, what is "Dust in the Wind"?
    a. everything
    b. your words of love
    c. gold and silver

35. According to the Mamas and the Papas in "Creeque Alley," as their career started no one was getting fat except _____.
    a. their agent
    b. McGuinn and McGuire
    c. Mama Cass

36. In "Band on the Run," where are Paul McCartney and Wings stuck?
    a. in your heart
    b. on a road to your door
    c. inside four walls

37. In "We Will Rock You," what does Queen say you're doing while you're playing in the street with mud on your face?
    a. messing up the place
    b. drawing a crowd
    c. kicking a can

38. In "It's a Beautiful Morning," what do the Young Rascals say the children will be there with?

    a. their schoolbooks
    b. red balloons
    c. robins and flowers

39. When Sly and the Family Stone say "I Want to Take You Higher," what do they want you to do to them?
    a. get them stoned
    b. light their fire
    c. go mountain biking

40. Where was Janis Joplin waiting for a train before becoming part of the traveling couple "Me and Bobby McGee"?
    a. Baton Rouge
    b. Cheyenne
    c. Tuscaloosa

41. In "Black Dog," what does Led Zeppelin say about a big-legged woman?
    a. she's got no soul
    b. she's hard to run away from
    c. she's the kind they'd like to meet

42. According to Tommy Roe, who gave the nickname to "Sweet Pea"?
    a. her teacher
    b. Popeye
    c. her friends

43. In "Long Time," what does Boston say you'll do after they've been gone?
    a. forget about them
    b. say you're sorry
    c. spread vicious rumors about them

44. Why won't Neil Diamond need bright lights when he is with "Cherry, Cherry"?
    a. because they'll make their own lightning
    b. because she looks better in the dark

    c. because his heart is already ablaze

45. Because they are "Paranoid," how does Black Sabbath describe what love is to them?
    a. it's frightening
    b. it's good and it's bad
    c. it's so unreal

46. Which city does Lou Reed say is the place to "Walk on the Wild Side"?
    a. Miami, FLA
    b. L.A.
    c. New York City

47. What do Alive and Kicking want you to do "Tighter, Tighter"?
    a. save money
    b. make love to them
    c. hold on

48. In "Let's Dance," what does David Bowie want you to put on?
    a. some clothes
    b. your red shoes
    c. your tight blue jeans

49. In "Here Comes My Baby," the Tremeloes aren't surprised that she's coming with _____.
    a. the smile of love
    b. a mask on her face
    c. another guy

50. Although a thousand other guys say they love you, what does the Association say, in "Cherish," that they only want to do?
    a. make you cry
    b. take you into the backseat and score
    c. gaze into your eyes

51. What does Traffic want "Dear Mr. Fantasy" to do for them to make them happy?

   a. take them aboard his magic swirling ship
   b. play a tune for them
   c. roll them a joint

52. According to Thin Lizzy, now that "The Boys Are Back in Town," where will they be hanging out?
   a. on street corners and at bus stops
   b. at the pool halls
   c. at Dino's Bar and Grill

53. At what time does "Gloria" come to Them's house?
   a. whenever she feels like it
   b. 7:00 P.M.
   c. around midnight

54. In "Mellow Yellow," what does Donovan say is going to be a sudden craze?
   a. sunflowers and moonbeams
   b. walking on the beach at sunset
   c. electrical bananas

55. Why do the Searchers say to "Don't Throw Your Love Away"?
   a. because any love is good love
   b. you might need it someday
   c. the land is already littered enough

56. In "You Ain't Seen Nothin' Yet," who did Bachman-Turner Overdrive go to see about a cure?
   a. their brother
   b. the doctor
   c. you

57. In "Running on Empty," Jackson Browne says you've got to do what you can to _____.
   a. keep your love alive
   b. make your dreams come true
   c. prove that you're still a man

58. In "Dream On," what does Aerosmith say may happen tomorrow?

    a. the good Lord will take you away
    b. your life may turn into a dream
    c. the sun will chase the clouds away

59. In "Love Takes Time," when Orleans saw a shooting star blaze a path across the sky, what did they also notice?
    a. it formed a twinkle in your eye
    b. it was followed closely by a U.F.O.
    c. the beauty did not last

60. When you have "Fame," what does David Bowie say you don't have?
    a. tomorrow
    b. a life of your own
    c. real friends

61. According to the Beatles in "Strawberry Fields Forever," under what conditions is living easy?
    a. when you're in love
    b. with eyes closed
    c. when the records are selling

62. Before they met "Lola," what hadn't the Kinks ever done before?
    a. seen the light
    b. kissed a woman
    c. gone to a nightclub

63. In "Don't Do Me Like That," what did a friend tell Tom Petty and the Heartbreakers that someone was going to do to them?
    a. tell them lies and cut them down to size
    b. spread rumors about their girl and try to run their world
    c. kick them around

64. What does Pink Floyd call "Money"?
    a. a poor man's treasure

    b. a gas

    c. a one-way street

65. Foreigner says that you're playing "Head Games" because you won't do what?

    a. show how you feel

    b. give it to them

    c. leave your other lover

66. Where does Jimi Hendrix want to take his "Foxy Lady"?

    a. to the dance

    b. on a trip

    c. home

67. What do Jan and Dean hear their favorite station's deejay say about "Drag City" races?

    a. they're a drag

    b. they're the fastest in the nation

    c. they're happening now

68. What's the name of Elton John's girlfriend in "Crocodile Rock"?

    a. Suzie

    b. Jeannie

    c. Ruby

69. Who is Brownsville Station "Smokin' in the Boy's Room" with?

    a. Frank and Paul

    b. the teachers

    c. the schoolyard junkies

70. In "Happy Together," what do the Turtles say you tell them that eases their mind?

    a. you don't mind if they see other girls

    b. you'll never leave

    c. you belong to them

71. According to Elvis Presley in "Mean Woman Blues," his woman is so mean, what does he compare her to?

   a. himself
   b. a junkyard dog
   c. a bitch in heat

72. Because they were "Lost in Love," what did Air Supply find out that they needed?
   a. a cure for their addiction
   b. someone to show them
   c. a prayer

73. What do the Animals tell their girlfriend in "We Gotta Get Out of This Place"?
   a. there's a better life for you and them
   b. life is what you make of it
   c. there's nothing a person can do about his life

74. According to the Beach Boys in "Fun, Fun, Fun," where did the girl cruise to in her T-Bird?
   a. the hamburger stand
   b. the beach
   c. the library

75. What did Neil Young do with his baby "Down by the River"?
   a. he kissed her
   b. he wrote a song with her
   c. he shot her

76. As the "Back Door Man," what do the Doors say they eat more of than any man has ever seen?
   a. Spam
   b. black-eyed peas
   c. chicken

77. According to Blondie in "Rapture," who comes down from the sky?
   a. the sky pilot
   b. a man from Mars
   c. lovers in moonbeams

78. In "That's All!," what did Genesis find out just when they thought everything was going all right?
    a. that love wasn't what it was cracked up to be
    b. that they were wrong
    c. that your plans didn't include them

79. Though "Good Girls Don't," what does the Knack add?
    a. they do
    b. they're not girls
    c. you're not good

80. What happens to the Mamas and the Papas upon the arrival of "Monday, Monday"?
    a. they start crying
    b. they can't wait for Friday
    c. they feel happy inside

81. According to the Police in "Wrapped Around Your Finger," what do you consider them?
    a. a young apprentice
    b. a pain in your side
    c. a prophet

82. In "Night Moves," what did Bob Seger awake last night to?
    a. the sound of a barking dog
    b. a dream that seemed so real
    c. the sound of thunder

83. What does Journey say they want to do when the "Lights" go down in the city and the sun shines on the bay?
    a. be there
    b. leave while there's still time
    c. pick up their guitars and play

84. What does Frank Zappa do that makes him a "Dancin' Fool"?
    a. he wears tights and a tutu

b. he plays music only for the money

c. he commits social suicide

85. What does It's a Beautiful Day say the "White Bird" must do?

    a. fly

    b. get some color into its life

    c. find a mate

86. In "Radar Love," the hands of Golden Earring are wet from doing what all night?

    a. crying

    b. driving

    c. washing dishes

87. What is it that you tell the Raspberries that makes them know you want to "Go All the Way"?

    a. that it's too early to go home now

    b. that they're the type of guy you've always dreamed about

    c. that it feels so right being with them tonight

88. After he rocks on through "Electric Avenue," what does Eddy Grant say he'll do?

    a. take it higher

    b. rock on through one more time

    c. bring all he's got to you

89. After they "Rock and Roll All Nite," what does Kiss want to do all day?

    a. sleep it off

    b. tan under the sun

    c. party

90. In "Isn't It Time," what was the last thing on the Babys' mind?

    a. that you weren't true

    b. that you were leaving

    c. falling in love

91. In "Hello, It's Me," what does Todd Rundgren take for granted?

    a. that life will never reveal its mystery to him

    b. that your telephone is always busy

    c. that you're always there but just don't care

92. What do your "Ebony Eyes" have Bob Welch hoping?

    a. that he'll be the vision of your happiness

    b. that he'll be holding you close tonight

    c. that you'll meet him under starry skies

93. Because you're a "Heartbreaker," what does Pat Benatar say your love has done to her?

    a. set her soul on fire

    b. made her go insane

    c. made her strong and free

94. What do Dion and the Belmonts ask the stars each night in "A Teenager in Love"?

    a. Why must they be a teenager in love?

    b. Where can they find another teenager in love?

    c. Why is there a law against being a teenager in love?

95. What does David Bowie feel like without his "China Girl"?

    a. free but lonely

    b. a wreck

    c. a man without a country

96. In "Burnin' for You," what does Blue Öyster Cult say is the essence and the season?

    a. time

    b. love

    c. rock and roll music

97. What does Supertramp say you're "Bloody Well Right" that it all depends on?

    a. money

    b. the love you share
    c. the hand of fate

98. Where did the Grateful Dead see their "Sugar Magnolia"?
    a. growing in the fields
    b. in a crowd of strangers
    c. down by the river

99. What is their "Centerfold" wearing that is really too much for the J. Geils Band?
    a. their jockey shorts
    b. a negligee
    c. nothing but a smile

100. In "Roundabout," who does Yes say is searching down on the land and catching the swirling wind?
    a. the Wicked Witch of the West
    b. the eagle
    c. the keeper of the sands of time

Hit Me With Your Best Shot
LEVEL FOUR

1. In "Heat of the Moment," what is it that Asia never meant to do?
   a. get turned on to you
   b. say goodbye and walk away
   c. be bad to you

2. Who was hiding in the corner during Rick Nelson's "Garden Party"?
   a. Jack
   b. Mr. Hughes
   c. John Lennon

3. In "So in to You," what did Atlanta Rhythm Section feel as they walked into the room?
   a. heavy breathing
   b. voodoo
   c. the stare of all the eyes

4. In "I Get Around," why do the Beach Boys always take their car?
   a. because the buses don't run after 12:00
   b. because it's the most boss car in the neighborhood
   c. because it's never been beat

5. What do the Beatles want you to "Tell Me Why"?
   a. why you left them
   b. why your shoes never match
   c. why you lied to them

6. In "No More Mr. Nice Guy," what does Alice Cooper say he used to be?

    a. a sweet thing

    b. a junkyard dog

    c. a pushover for pretty girls

7. In "Travelin' Band," what did Creedence Clearwater Revival say they had to do when someone got excited?

    a. move to another town

    b. call the state militia

    c. play a little louder

8. According to Bob Dylan in "Positively 4th Street," what did you do when he was down?

    a. you helped him up

    b. you stood there grinning

    c. you knelt down beside him

9. In "Midnight Confessions," why do the Grass Roots feel they are wasting their time in pursuing their love interest?

    a. you don't even know they exist

    b. you won't prove your love to them

    c. you're already attached

10. According to Daryl Hall and John Oates, what is it that "You Make My Dreams" do?

    a. always return to you

    b. turn misty blue

    c. come true

11. Although it is commonly thought that "Everybody Loves a Clown," Gary Lewis and the Playboys ask __.

    a. Are they the exception?

    b. Is there a deeper reason why clowns exist?

    c. Why don't you love clowns?

12. In "D'yer Maker," what does Led Zeppelin say you don't have to do?

    a. pretend that you still care

    b. go

   c. keep on breaking their heart

13. According to Kiss in "I Was Made for Lovin' You," when do they plan to make it all come true?

   a. when they're finally alone with you
   b. tonight
   c. after the dance

14. What does John Cougar Mellencamp say about his "Small Town"?

   a. it's good enough for him
   b. it's filled with small people who use small words
   c. it's a place to make you crazy

15. According to Wings in "Listen to What the Man Said," what can you hear the people say?

   a. rumors, lies, and alibis
   b. that there's nothing you can do that can't be done
   c. that love is blind

16. What does the Steve Miller Band say they have to be while they're "Living in the U.S.A."?

   a. rock and roll stars
   b. free
   c. happy

17. In "Jump," where does Van Halen want you to notice them standing?

   a. on the dance floor
   b. in the water
   c. by the record machine

18. How does Queen describe the "Killer Queen"?

   a. as dynamite with a laser beam
   b. as a real hot cookie with a sting of love
   c. as steroids with a bad attitude

19. Freddy Cannon says that, when you're at "Palisades Park," you'll never know how great it can feel unless you stop _____.

    a. in the middle of the mountain of love
    b. after eating a nine-course meal
    c. at the top of the Ferris wheel

20. Because they're a "Long, Long Way From Home," even amidst a million faces how does Foreigner feel?
    a. like a foreigner
    b. like a wayward pioneer
    c. alone

21. What does King Harvest say you can't be if you're "Dancin' in the Moonlight"?
    a. standing still
    b. square
    c. uptight

22. When they pass "Linda" on the street, what happens to Jan and Dean?
    a. they get slapped silly
    b. they can't speak
    c. their heart skips a beat

23. In "Walk Away," what does the James Gang say you don't want to do?
    a. admit that you were wrong
    b. talk about it
    c. compromise

24. In "I Can't Hold Back," what does Survivor feel is reaching out to both them and you?
    a. the power of love
    b. the long arm of the law
    c. the hand of fate

25. In "Immigrant Song," where does Led Zeppelin say they come from?
    a. the gutters and the slums
    b. any place they're not wanted
    c. the land of ice and snow

26. According to the Tremeloes in "Silence Is Golden," what is cheap and makes people follow like sheep?
   a. sex
   b. talk
   c. a fancy reputation

27. Donovan, the "Sunshine Superman," says he'll pick up your hand and then _____.
   a. blow your mind
   b. kiss your cares away
   c. run it through his hair

28. In "Willow Weep for Me," to whom do Chad and Jeremy want the willow to whisper that love has sinned?
   a. to a friend
   b. to the wind
   c. to you

29. In "(Don't Fear) the Reaper," what does Blue Öyster Cult say you'll be able to do if you take their hand?
   a. read their mind
   b. dream
   c. fly

30. In "The Ballad of Easy Rider," where do the Byrds say they want to be?
   a. in the saddle of a motorcycle
   b. wherever the river flows
   c. in your arms

31. What do the Rolling Stones say will happen to them if someone doesn't "Gimme Shelter"?
   a. they're going to fade away
   b. they'll live out on the streets
   c. they'll find a way to get even one day

32. What does Patrick Simmons say can be "So Wrong"?
   a. love

    b. your promises

    c. people's trust in one another

33. Because they are "Bad Company," what does Bad Company say they were born with?

    a. dragon breath

    b. a chip on their shoulder and a bad attitude

    c. a six-gun in their hand

34. What does Jackson Browne say he's going to do to "Somebody's Baby"?

    a. walk up to her and talk to her

    b. steal her heart away

    c. make her cry

35. What are Ten Years After "Goin' Home" to do?

    a. take a shower

    b. catch up on what they've been missing

    c. get you

36. What does Jimi Hendrix call his "Manic Depression"?

    a. a great way to get down

    b. a frustrating mess

    c. nothing more than a state of mind

37. Why are Herman's Hermits "Leaning on a Lamp Post"?

    a. they're waiting for the evening to arrive

    b. they are waiting for a lady to come by

    c. they're out to steal a car

38. Although their girlfriend is no longer there, what is so strong for Tommy James and the Shondells that makes their "Mirage" seem so real?

    a. her perfume

    b. their imagination

    c. their love

39. What does Lynyrd Skynyrd say the "Saturday Night Special" is good for?

    a. a lot of laughs and a whole lot of fun

    b. nothing except to put a man six feet in a hole
    c. seeing the world with a new point of view

40. The Jefferson Airplane say that you'll need "Somebody to Love" when the truth is found to be _____.

    a. just a dream
    b. absent
    c. lies

41. When did Manfred Mann sing "Sha La La"?
    a. the night they first met you
    b. when they took a shower
    c. when you asked them to marry you

42. According to Paul McCartney in "Another Day," although the man of the girl's dreams comes to break her spell of living alone, how long does he stay?
    a. one night
    b. a week
    c. until she chases a new dream

43. According to Emerson, Lake and Palmer, what was meant "From the Beginning"?
    a. you were meant to be here
    b. rock was meant to rule
    c. hearts were meant to be broken

44. What did Warren Zevon see one of the "Werewolves of London" doing at Trader Vic's?
    a. drinking a piña colada
    b. looking for victims
    c. chatting with a lady of the night

45. In the Trade Winds' "New York's a Lonely Town," it is such a long way from Jackson Park to where?
    a. Pasadena
    b. Pomona
    c. Shreveport

46. Terry Stafford has "Suspicion" that, every time you kiss him, he's not certain whether _____.

   a. you love him
   b. you know who you're with
   c. he's good enough for you

47. According to the J. Geils Band in "Give It to Me," what is too good to hide?

   a. your face
   b. your love
   c. your diary

48. In "Journey to the Center of the Mind," the Amboy Dukes invite you to take a ride to the land _____.

   a. of love
   b. of make-believe
   c. inside your mind

49. In "Friday on My Mind," what will the Easybeats do when Friday evening comes along?

   a. go to a movie
   b. spend all their money
   c. get drunk

50. In "Tiny Dancer," who does Elton John see in the streets?

   a. fans and groupies
   b. images of former rock and roll greats
   c. Jesus freaks

51. In "Head First," what are the Babys and their girl doing tonight?

   a. saying goodbye
   b. going out
   c. making love

52. David Essex wants you to "Rock On" by doing what?

   a. snapping your fingers and stomping your feet
   b. shaking your head while wiggling your toes

    c. jumping up and down in your blue suede shoes

53. What are "Hot Girls in Love" doing that's a little too much for Loverboy?
    a. spending all his cash
    b. leaving him out of the action
    c. turning on the heat

54. Because they're "Bad to the Bone," what do George Thorogood and the Destroyers say they broke before they met you?
    a. every plate in the house
    b. a thousand hearts
    c. every rule in the book

55. In "Travelin' Man," who makes Ricky Nelson's heart start to yearn?
    a. you do
    b. his fräulein in Berlin
    c. his china doll in Hong Kong

56. The Ides of March say that, if you want to be a movie star, they'll take you in their "Vehicle" to _____.
    a. Burbank
    b. Miami Beach
    c. Hollywood

57. Along with "Orange Skies," what two other things does Love associate with the warm feeling of being with you?
    a. sunshine and lollipops
    b. carnivals and cotton candy
    c. cornbread and muffins

58. "On the Way Home," the Buffalo Springfield claim that though we rush ahead to save our time, _____.
    a. we are only what we feel
    b. our goals slip farther away
    c. we measure what we've lost

59. On what day is it that the Fortunes always seem to feel "Here Comes That Rainy Day Feeling Again"?
   a. Friday
   b. Sunday
   c. Monday

60. According to Gary U.S. Bonds, what is every Southern belle down in "New Orleans"?
   a. a real humdinger
   b. a Mississippi queen
   c. a Southern man's delight

61. According to Sir Douglas Quintet in "She's About a Mover," what do you need to have the perfect relationship?
   a. trust
   b. a lot of luck
   c. conversation

62. According to the Surfaris, at what surf spot did "Surfer Joe" hang five, walk the nose, and win the trophy?
   a. Huntington Beach
   b. Malibu
   c. Pipeline

63. According to Bob Dylan, who are the "Chimes of Freedom" tolling for?
   a. every hung-up person
   b. you and me and liberty
   c. the churches in the land

64. In "L.A. Woman," how long ago did the Doors say they arrived in town?
   a. a week ago
   b. a year ago
   c. about an hour ago

65. In "1984," what does Spirit say you should start thinking about doing?

   a. fighting back
   b. planning for your future
   c. raising a family

66. According to Roxy Music in "Love Is the Drug," what happens after they say "Go" and she says "Yes"?
   a. their folks say "No"
   b. they dim the lights
   c. the next few words are hard to resist

67. In "Renegade," who does Styx say is coming down to greet them?
   a. their baby
   b. the grim reaper
   c. the hangman

68. In "Just a Song Before I Go," what do Crosby, Stills and Nash say it's easy to do when you're traveling twice the speed of sound?
   a. lose track of simple things
   b. get burned
   c. see the world spinning before you

69. In "Show Me the Way," how does Peter Frampton feel he's swimming?
   a. like a lemming
   b. as if he's blindfolded
   c. in a circle

70. What does Eddie Money plan to do with you with his "Two Tickets to Paradise"?
   a. disappear
   b. make things better
   c. take a trip to never-never land

71. Because you're a "Heartbreaker," now that you've taught Pat Benatar the ways of desire, what has happened?
   a. you've let her go

    b. it's taken its toll on her

    c. she's learned how to be a heartbreaker, too

72. In "Rock On," what does David Essex wonder?

    a. Where do we go from here?

    b. Whatever happened to the beat?

    c. Will time make man more wise?

73. In "God Save the Queen," what do the Sex Pistols say they are?

    a. the future

    b. citizens of the world

    c. a bunch of freaked-out druggies

74. Where is ZZ Top looking for some "Tush"?

    a. in bars and dirty alleys

    b. in Dallas and Hollywood

    c. in Philadelphia and St. Paul

75. What will the Who do in hopes we "Won't Get Fooled Again"?

    a. play their music loud and free

    b. dream like kids but act like men

    c. get down on their knees and pray

76. In "Well All Right," what does Blind Faith say they'll do with all their might?

    a. learn to treat you right

    b. convince you to let them stay overnight

    c. live and love

77. What do Frank Zappa and the Mothers of Invention reply when asking "What's the Ugliest Part of Your Body"?

    a. your mind

    b. your name

    c. your self

78. According to Bad Company in "Shooting Star," what was the first Beatles' song that Johnny heard?

    a. "Helter Skelter"
    b. "Get Back"
    c. "Love Me Do"

79. In "Never Been to Spain," Three Dog Night also admit they've never been to England but that they kinda like the _____.
    a. Beatles
    b. Queen
    c. music

80. In "Soul Deep," if you should leave the Boxtops, what would they simply be?
    a. alone and blue
    b. happy and free
    c. an empty shell

81. When everything is finished, how does Van Morrison say you'll be living with all your "Blue Money"?
    a. in clover
    b. you'll be feeling blue all over
    c. high in the sky

82. In "Every Little Thing She Does Is Magic," even though their life is full of tragic events, what do the Police say about their love for her?
    a. it goes on
    b. it's a mystery
    c. it's the biggest tragedy of all

83. Why does Jimi Hendrix say you're just like "Crosstown Traffic"?
    a. because you're always changing your signals
    b. because it's so hard to get through to you
    c. because you're always causing problems

84. The Kinks ask you to "Set Me Free" under what condition?
    a. if you won't let them date other girls

b. under no conditions

c. if they can't have you to themselves

85. According to the Rolling Stones in "Bitch," what do they do when you call their name?

    a. heat up like a burning flame

    b. salivate like a Pavlov dog

    c. run for the nearest shelter

86. According to Mott the Hoople, what does the television man say "All the Young Dudes" are?

    a. the future of rock and roll

    b. Casanovas in beggars' clothing

    c. juvenile delinquent wrecks

87. What does the Electric Light Orchestra say they've got to do with their "Sweet Talkin' Woman"?

    a. tame her down

    b. get back to her

    c. keep listening to her sweet lies

88. In "Take It to the Limit," because the dreams they've seen lately are turning out the same, what do the Eagles want you to do?

    a. put them on a highway and show them a sign

    b. march to a different drummer

    c. cast away their doubts so they can live without jealousy

89. In "Wishing You Were Here," what does Chicago say they'd do just to be with you tonight?

    a. change their life

    b. rob, cheat, and steal

    c. climb the highest mountain

90. In "Come On Down to My Boat," what is the name of Every Mother's Son's latest female catch?

    a. Barbara Ann

    b. Gertrude

   c. they don't know her name

91. Although "Some Guys Have All the Luck," what does Rod Stewart say that some guys do all the time?
- **a.** chase the wrong girls
- **b.** complain
- **c.** brag about their trophies

92. What does Toto say they bless down in "Africa"?
- **a.** the rains
- **b.** the hearts of all the girls
- **c.** spiders and snakes

93. Steely Dan wonders whether you're "Reeling in the Years" and also _____.
- **a.** hiding all the tears
- **b.** stowing away the time
- **c.** planning your career

94. In "Born to Run," what does Bruce Springsteen call the town?
- **a.** a death trap
- **b.** Anytown, USA
- **c.** a place to fight the blues

95. What do the Raiders say their offbeat "Arizona" friend is acting like?
- **a.** a little devil
- **b.** a sly fox
- **c.** a teenybopper

96. Now that he's "Eighteen," what does Alice Cooper say he's got?
- **a.** a baby's brain and an old man's heart
- **b.** heartaches and pain
- **c.** raging hormones and a strong desire

97. According to Rush, who forge their creativity "Closer to the Heart"?
- **a.** the blacksmith and the artist

    b. lawyers and thieves

    c. those who have ever been in love

98. According to Pink Floyd in "Time," what is the English way?

    a. eating tea and crumpets with little to say

    b. hanging on in quiet desperation

    c. making every moment count before they turn old and grey

99. Supertramp says you should "Take the Long Way Home" if you think you're the part of whom in a picture show?

    a. the cowardly lion

    b. the Lone Ranger

    c. Romeo

100. What does the Grateful Dead say you can do with their "Box of Rain"?

    a. save it for a sunny day

    b. believe it if you need it or leave it if you dare

    c. let it bring drops of happiness when the world turns its back on you

IV

Name That Tune:
Classic Rock Title Questions

Take It Easy
LEVEL ONE

1. There's *a time to rend, a time to sow*.
   a. "Baby the Rain Must Fall"/Glenn Yarbrough
   b. "Turn! Turn! Turn!"/Byrds
   c. "Let's Dance"/Chris Montez

2. The rhythm section consisted of *the Purple Gang*.
   a. "Rock and Roll Heaven"/Righteous Brothers
   b. "I Fought the Law"/Bobby Fuller Four
   c. "Jailhouse Rock"/Elvis Presley

3. *The ink is black, the page is white*—and together we *learn to read and write*.
   a. "People Got to Be Free"/Rascals
   b. "Black and White"/Three Dog Night
   c. "Wonderful World"/Herman's Hermits

4. Because *you need coolin'*, they're going to *send you back to schoolin'*.
   a. "Whole Lotta Love"/Led Zeppelin
   b. "Go All the Way"/Raspberries
   c. "Layla"/Derek and the Dominos

5. *Listening to the teachers* just isn't their bag.
   a. "Smokin' in the Boy's Room"/Brownsville Station
   b. "Clap for the Wolfman"/Guess Who
   c. "Rock and Roll Music"/Beach Boys

6. They *left a good job in the city* working for the man every night and day.
   a. "Proud Mary"/Creedence Clearwater Revival
   b. "Friday on My Mind"/Easybeats

c. "Long Train Runnin'"/Doobie Brothers

7. She can *rely on the old man's money.*
   a. "Cat Scratch Fever"/Ted Nugent
   b. "Beth"/Kiss
   c. "Rich Girl"/Daryl Hall and John Oates

8. He claims *it was in self-defense.*
   a. "I Shot the Sheriff"/Eric Clapton
   b. "Alone Again (Naturally)"/Gilbert O'Sullivan
   c. "Space Oddity"/David Bowie

9. This is taking place *in the jungle, the mighty jungle.*
   a. "There's a Kind of Hush"/Herman's Hermits
   b. "Young Love"/Tab Hunter
   c. "The Lion Sleeps Tonight"/Tokens

10. *Some dance to remember, some dance to forget.*
    a. "Love Hurts"/Nazareth
    b. "Hotel California"/Eagles
    c. "Lonely People"/America

11. They'll *be watching every move you make.*
    a. "Every Breath You Take"/Police
    b. "Here I Am"/Air Supply
    c. "Hungry Like the Wolf"/Duran Duran

12. They were *making love in the green grass.*
    a. "I Think We're Alone Now"/Tommy James and the Shondells
    b. "Brown-Eyed Girl"/Van Morrison
    c. "Groovin'"/Young Rascals

13. All your money *won't another minute buy.*
    a. "More Than a Feeling"/Boston
    b. "Dream Weaver"/Gary Wright
    c. "Dust in the Wind"/Kansas

14. You never do anything *to save your doggone soul.*
    a. "Hound Dog"/Elvis Presley

    b. "Shake, Rattle and Roll"/Bill Haley and His Comets

    c. "That'll Be the Day"/Buddy Holly and the Crickets

15. They're surprised to see that *she's walking back to them.*

    a. "Oh, Pretty Woman"/Van Halen

    b. "Goodbye Stranger"/Supertramp

    c. "Come On Eileen"/Dexys Midnight Runners

16. Although they heard that you're leaving, they hope that maybe *you could have a change of heart.*

    a. "Billy, Don't Be a Hero"/Bo Donaldson and the Heywoods

    b. "Runaway"/Jefferson Starship

    c. "Rikki Don't Lose That Number"/Steely Dan

17. They *haven't done a bloody thing all day.*

    a. "Stuck in the Middle With You"/Stealers Wheel

    b. "I Just Want to Celebrate"/Rare Earth

    c. "Uncle Albert"/Paul and Linda McCartney

18. They'll *help you party down.*

    a. "We're an American Band"/Grand Funk Railroad

    b. "Get Down Tonight"/KC and the Sunshine Band

    c. "You Ain't Seen Nothin' Yet"/Bachman-Turner Overdrive

19. *Black as the dark night* she was.

    a. "Venus"/Bananarama

    b. "Angie"/Rolling Stones

    c. "Dancing Queen"/Abba

20. They drink champagne in the bar, and *it tastes just like cherry cola.*

    a. "Lola"/Kinks

    b. "Brandy"/Looking Glass

    c. "I Want Candy"/Strangeloves

21. He asks, *"Hey little sister, who's your superman?"*

    a. "Da Ya Think I'm Sexy"/Rod Stewart

    b. "White Wedding"/Billy Idol

    c. "Faith"/George Michael

22. *Life goes on long after the thrill of living is gone.*

    a. "Jack and Diane"/John Cougar

    b. "Reeling in the Years"/Steely Dan

    c. "Glory Days"/Bruce Springsteen

23. *The Byrds and the Jefferson Airplane flew* here.

    a. "San Francisco (Be Sure to Wear Flowers in Your Hair)"/Scott McKenzie

    b. "Eight Miles High"/Byrds

    c. "Monterey"/Eric Burdon and the Animals

24. They *don't need no education,* so they ask the teachers to *leave the kids alone.*

    a. "We Will Rock You"/Queen

    b. "Another Brick in the Wall"/Pink Floyd

    c. "Message in a Bottle"/Police

25. They're *leaving in the morning* and they *must see you again.*

    a. "Last Train to Clarksville"/Monkees

    b. "Leaving on a Jet Plane"/Peter, Paul and Mary

    c. "Workin' My Way Back to You"/Four Seasons

26. He wonders how it feels *to be on your own with no direction home.*

    a. "Like a Rolling Stone"/Bob Dylan

    b. "Eve of Destruction"/Barry McGuire

    c. "Secret Agent Man"/Johnny Rivers

27. You *don't have to read their mind* to know what they *have in mind.*

    a. "Hot Blooded"/Foreigner

    b. "Give a Little Bit"/Supertramp

    c. "Baby Come Back"/Player

28. They've been *for a walk on a winter's day.*

    a. "Lazy Day"/Spanky and Our Gang
    b. "The Sounds of Silence"/Simon and Garfunkel
    c. "California Dreamin'"/The Mamas and the Papas

29. Once you listen to rock and roll, *you can't wipe it off your face no matter how hard you try.*
    a. "Do You Believe in Magic"/Lovin' Spoonful
    b. "Rock and Roll Is Here to Stay"/Danny and the Juniors
    c. "Rock and Roll Music"/Beatles

30. By the time they arrived there, there were a half million people *in song and celebration.*
    a. "On the Road Again"/Canned Heat
    b. "Woodstock"/Crosby, Stills, Nash and Young
    c. "Joy to the World"/Three Dog Night

31. He says you could *have a steam train if you just lay down your tracks.*
    a. "I Want Your Sex"/George Michael
    b. "Sledgehammer"/Peter Gabriel
    c. "Roll With It"/Stevie Winwood

32. For them, *every day's the Fourth of July.*
    a. "Saturday in the Park"/Chicago
    b. "More Today Than Yesterday"/Spiral Starecase
    c. "At the Hop"/Danny and the Juniors

33. They hear *hurricanes a-blowin'* and fear the *rivers overflowin'.*
    a. "Stormy"/Classics IV
    b. "Bad Moon Rising"/Creedence Clearwater Revival
    c. "Ticket to Ride"/Beatles

34. Everything *looks so complete when you walk out on the street and the wind catches your feet.*
    a. "Summer Breeze"/Seals and Crofts
    b. "Morning Has Broken"/Cat Stevens
    c. "Wild Night"/Van Morrison

35. You can have it *if it makes you feel good.*
    a. "Sugar, Sugar"/Archies
    b. "Piece of My Heart"/Big Brother and the Holding Company
    c. "Hair"/Cowsills

36. Although you think *you've lost your love,* they've seen her and *it's you she's thinking of.*
    a. "Devoted to You"/Everly Brothers
    b. "Under My Thumb"/Rolling Stones
    c. "She Loves You"/Beatles

37. They *heard it from a friend who heard it from a friend* that *you've been messing around.*
    a. "Private Eyes"/Daryl Hall and John Oates
    b. "Who's Crying Now"/Journey
    c. "Take It on the Run"/REO Speedwagon

38. He will *try to express his inner feeling and thankfulness* for showing him *the meaning of success.*
    a. "Woman"/John Lennon
    b. "Blue Eyes"/Elton John
    c. "Sussudio"/Phil Collins

39. They say it's *easy to be proud* and just as *easy to say no.*
    a. "Indian Reservation"/Raiders
    b. "Easy to Be Hard"/Three Dog Night
    c. "Only in America"/Jay and the Americans

40. There's *only one cure for that body* of his, and that's *to have that girl that* he *loves so fine.*
    a. "Cherry Cherry"/Neil Diamond
    b. "All Shook Up"/Elvis Presley
    c. "Foxy Lady"/Jimi Hendrix

41. They *see Marianne walking away.*
    a. "Heartache Tonight"/Eagles

   b. "Don't Stop"/Fleetwood Mac
   c. "More Than a Feeling"/Boston
42. *The only thing a gambler needs is a suitcase and a trunk.*
   a. "The House of the Rising Sun"/Animals
   b. "Tumbling Dice"/Rolling Stones
   c. "Mr. Bojangles"/Nitty Gritty Dirt Band
43. She's *not the kind of girl who gives up just like that,* so she'll *wait until it's* her *turn.*
   a. "The Winner Takes It All"/Abba
   b. "Treat Me Right"/Pat Benatar
   c. "The Tide Is High"/Blondie
44. They'd *pay the devil to replace her.*
   a. "So in to You"/Atlanta Rhythm Section
   b. "Fallin' in Love"/Hamilton, Joe Frank and Reynolds
   c. "She's Gone"/Daryl Hall and John Oates
45. They *want* their *MTV.*
   a. "Girls on Film"/Duran Duran
   b. "Money for Nothing"/Dire Straits
   c. "Video Killed the Radio Star"/Buggles
46. They told their doctor that *they got the fever; you got the cure.*
   a. "Gimme Some Lovin'"/Spencer Davis Group
   b. "Love Potion Number Nine"/Searchers
   c. "Good Lovin'"/Young Rascals
47. They're *not trying to cause a big sensation.*
   a. "My Generation"/Who
   b. "Revolution"/Beatles
   c. "(I Can't Get No) Satisfaction"/Rolling Stones
48. *There's no hell below us, and above us, only sky.*
   a. "Spirit in the Sky"/Norman Greenbaum
   b. "What the World Needs Now Is Love"/Jackie DeShannon

    c. "Imagine"/John Lennon

49. People come to *Waimea Bay* to ride those *waves, some thirty feet high.*
    a. "Ride the Wild Surf"/Jan and Dean
    b. "Surfin' U.S.A."/Beach Boys
    c. "Wipeout"/Surfaris

50. Because she's *sure all that glitters is gold,* she's *buying* it.
    a. "Stairway to Heaven"/Led Zeppelin
    b. "Heart of Gold"/Neil Young
    c. "Seasons in the Sun"/Terry Jacks

51. They say that *it's your life and you can do what you want* to do.
    a. "Tired of Waiting for You"/Kinks
    b. "It's My Life"/Animals
    c. "It Ain't Me Babe"/Turtles

52. They tell you to say this *if the ever-changing world in which we live in makes you give in and cry.*
    a. "One Toke Over the Line"/Brewer and Shipley
    b. "Live and Let Die"/Wings
    c. "I Just Want to Celebrate"/Rare Earth

53. They want you to *pick up the beat* and *kick up your feet.*
    a. "Moonlight Feels Right"/Starbuck
    b. "Dust in the Wind"/Kansas
    c. "Dance With Me"/Orleans

54. They want you to *c'mon and let it show.*
    a. "Love Is All Around"/Troggs
    b. "Come On Up"/Young Rascals
    c. "Louie, Louie"/Kingsmen

55. *At the end of the rainbow is a golden oldie.*
    a. "Life Is a Rock"/Reunion
    b. "Fly Like an Eagle"/Steve Miller Band

    c. "Old Time Rock and Roll"/Bob Seger and the Silver Bullet Band

56. They say you *led them to believe you're old enough to give* them *love.*
    a. "Young Girl"/Gary Puckett and the Union Gap
    b. "Big Girls Don't Cry"/Four Seasons
    c. "It's All Over Now"/Rolling Stones

57. He sees himself as *a lonely man in the middle of something* he *doesn't really understand.*
    a. "It Don't Come Easy"/Ringo Starr
    b. "Imagine"/John Lennon
    c. "Maybe I'm Amazed"/Paul McCartney

58. Everybody is *feeling warm and right* because it's *such a fine and natural sight.*
    a. "Nights in White Satin"/Moody Blues
    b. "Morning Has Broken"/Cat Stevens
    c. "Dancing in the Moonlight"/King Harvest

59. *Where are you going with that gun in your hand?*
    a. "War"/Edwin Starr
    b. "Hey Joe"/Jimi Hendrix
    c. "I Fought the Law"/Bobby Fuller Four

60. There's a girl they know *who makes* them *feel so good,* and they *wouldn't live without her even if* they *could.*
    a. "Valleri"/Monkees
    b. "Darlin'"/Beach Boys
    c. "Hang On Sloopy"/McCoys

61. They like to *work at nothing all day.*
    a. "Taking Care of Business"/Bachman-Turner Overdrive
    b. "Games"/Redeye
    c. "Rock'n Me"/Steve Miller Band

62. She's *bending down to give* them *a rainbow.*
    a. "She's a Rainbow"/Rolling Stones

    b. "Windy"/Association
    c. "Mrs. Robinson"/Simon and Garfunkel

63. You *pull up to a drive-in and find a place to park*; you *hop into the back seat where you know it's nice and dark.*
    a. "No Particular Place to Go"/Chuck Berry
    b. "Your Mama Don't Dance"/Loggins and Messina
    c. "Rave On"/Buddy Holly and the Crickets

64. The *Ukraine girls* really knock them out.
    a. "California Girls"/Beach Boys
    b. "Back in the USSR"/Beatles
    c. "Marrakesh Express"/Crosby, Stills and Nash

65. Washing their face after making love in the afternoon, they return to find *someone else was taking* their *place.*
    a. "You've Lost That Lovin' Feeling"/Righteous Brothers
    b. "I Wonder What She's Doing Tonite"/Tommy Boyce and Bobby Hart
    c. "Cecilia"/Simon and Garfunkel

66. *Get your motor running* and *head out on the highway.*
    a. "Born to Be Wild"/Steppenwolf
    b. "I'm Free"/Who
    c. "Little Honda"/Hondells

67. He asks you not to *deny your man's desire* because *ain't nobody gonna stop him now.*
    a. "Bad Case of Loving You"/Robert Palmer
    b. "Tonight's the Night"/Rod Stewart
    c. "White Wedding"/Billy Idol

68. They want her to *ease* their *worried mind.*
    a. "Layla"/Derek and the Dominos
    b. "Witchy Woman"/Eagles

    c. "Black Magic Woman"/Santana

69. They see *faded photographs* covered *with lines and creases.*

    a. "One"/Three Dog Night

    b. "Kind of a Drag"/Buckinghams

    c. "Traces"/Classics IV

70. He wants you to do this because he *can't remember.*

    a. "Let's Dance"/David Bowie

    b. "Take Me Home"/Phil Collins

    c. "Make Me Lose Control"/Eric Carmen

71. They know that they must do what's right *sure as Kilimanjaro rises like a leopardess above the Serengeti.*

    a. "Africa"/Toto

    b. "Keep On Loving You"/REO Speedwagon

    c. "Every Woman in the World"/Air Supply

72. You'll be their *loving woman and* they'll *be your loving man.*

    a. "Let's Live for Today"/Grass Roots

    b. "Game of Love"/Wayne Fontana and the Mindbenders

    c. "All My Lovin'"/Beatles

73. *She gets to know you, and she goes to own you.*

    a. "Dominique"/Singing Nun

    b. "Runaround Sue"/Dion

    c. "Kentucky Woman"/Neil Diamond

74. They say you're a *disgrace* because you've got *blood all over your face* and you're *waving your banner all over the place.*

    a. "Stayin' Alive"/Bee Gees

    b. "Don't Bring Me Down"/Electric Light Orchestra

    c. "We Will Rock You"/Queen

75. They *take whatever* they *want,* and now they *want you.*

    a. "Tush"/ZZ Top
    b. "Can't Get Enough"/Bad Company
    c. "Come and Get Your Love"/Redbone

76. They're *the young generation* and they've *got something to say.*
    a. "Over Under Sideways Down"/Yardbirds
    b. "My Generation"/Who
    c. "Monkees Theme"/Monkees

77. *The bird is the word.*
    a. "There Has to Be a Word"/Innocents
    b. "The Word"/Beatles
    c. "Surfin' Bird"/Trashmen

78. He was ten years old when he first got it, *from some kitty next door.*
    a. "Life's Been Good"/Joe Walsh
    b. "Cat Scratch Fever"/Ted Nugent
    c. "Night Moves"/Bob Seger

79. The *three men* he admired most *caught the last train for the coast.*
    a. "Abraham, Martin and John"/Dion
    b. "American Pie"/Don McLean
    c. "Please Come to Boston"/Dave Loggins

80. It breaks her heart to find that she's given her love *to a man whose hands are cold as ice.*
    a. "Cold as Ice"/Foreigner
    b. "Lyin' Eyes"/Eagles
    c. "Rich Girl"/Daryl Hall and John Oates

81. Because *yesterday's gone,* they recommend for you to think *about tomorrow.*
    a. "Let Your Love Flow"/Bellamy Brothers
    b. "Don't Stop"/Fleetwood Mac
    c. "Dream On"/Aerosmith

82. She's got *electric boots* and *a mohair suit.*

    a. "Gypsy Woman"/Brian Hyland
    b. "Benny and the Jets"/Elton John
    c. "My Maria"/B. W. Stevenson

83. They've *got a good reason for taking the easy way out.*
    a. "Because"/Dave Clark Five
    b. "The Last Time"/Rolling Stones
    c. "Day Tripper"/Beatles

84. They ask her to *think what the future would be with a poor boy* like them.
    a. "Just Once in My Life"/Righteous Brothers
    b. "Wouldn't It Be Nice"/Beach Boys
    c. "Dawn"/Four Seasons

85. Drive-in movies and *Howdy Doody* and other memories *seem like yesterday.*
    a. "Hooked on a Feeling"/Blue Swede
    b. "Old Days"/Chicago
    c. "At Seventeen"/Janis Ian

86. They *hang your picture on the wall* to *hide a nasty stain that's lying there.*
    a. "I'm Not in Love"/10cc
    b. "Beth"/Kiss
    c. "Why Can't We Be Friends?"/War

87. All they need *is a drummer for people who only need a beat.*
    a. "Dance to the Music"/Sly and the Family Stone
    b. "Tighten Up"/Archie Bell and the Drells
    c. "I Got Rhythm"/Happenings

88. They're *trying to make a living and doing the best* they *can.*
    a. "Ramblin' Man"/Allman Brothers Band
    b. "Taking Care of Business"/Bachman-Turner Overdrive
    c. "Stuck in the Middle With You"/Stealers Wheel

89. He's *too young to be singing the blues.*
  a. "Sunshine"/Jonathan Edwards
  b. "Goodbye Yellow Brick Road"/Elton John
  c. "Rock On"/David Essex

90. Once you're in him, you *start eating cars: Cadillacs, Lincolns, Mercuries and Subarus.*
  a. "Rapture"/Blondie
  b. "Pac-Man Fever"/Buckner and Garcia
  c. "Maniac"/Michael Sembello

91. *When the pain of love surrounds you,* they'll *take you far away from this place and time.*
  a. "You're the Only Woman"/Ambrosia
  b. "Count on Me"/Jefferson Starship
  c. "Don't Look Back"/Boston

92. *Nothing is real.*
  a. "No Time"/Guess Who
  b. "Mirage"/Tommy James and the Shondells
  c. "Strawberry Fields Forever"/Beatles

93. She makes them *feel like a river.*
  a. "My Woman From Tokyo"/Deep Purple
  b. "Lola"/Kinks
  c. "Brandy"/Looking Glass

94. They want you to *help* them *get around to their heart.*
  a. "Help Me Girl"/Animals
  b. "Help Me, Rhonda"/Beach Boys
  c. "Help!"/Beatles

95. They say that *you'd think those people would have had enough* of them, but when they look around, they see *it isn't so.*
  a. "Silly Love Songs"/Wings
  b. "Dreams"/Fleetwood Mac
  c. "Nights in White Satin"/Moody Blues

96. He's got to take his *problems to the United Nations.*

     a. "Summertime Blues"/Eddie Cochran
     b. "Teen-Age Idol"/Rick Nelson
     c. "A Teenager in Love"/Dion and the Belmonts

97. Although she makes him *nervous and scared,* he'd feel so good if he could *say the word.*
     a. "Sorry Seems to Be the Hardest Word"/Elton John
     b. "Sussudio"/Phil Collins
     c. "I Wanna Be Your Lover"/Prince

98. They say you *lay still in the grass coiled up and hissing.*
     a. "Love Hurts"/Nazareth
     b. "Keep On Loving You"/REO Speedwagon
     c. "Maneater"/Daryl Hall and John Oates

99. *In the midnight hour, she cries "more, more, more."*
     a. "Roxanne"/Police
     b. "Rebel Yell"/Billy Idol
     c. "Rio"/Duran Duran

100. She was *working for the F.B.I.*
     a. "Lovely Rita"/Beatles
     b. "Maggie May"/Rod Stewart
     c. "Long Cool Woman"/Hollies

Who Can It Be Now?
LEVEL TWO

1. They *tried to make it on Sunday* but they *got so damn depressed.*
   a. "Strange Way"/Firefall
   b. "Long, Long Way From Home"/Foreigner
   c. "Sister Golden Hair"/America

2. They want you to *let your hair down,* let your hair down on them.
   a. "Lady Godiva"/Peter and Gordon
   b. "Hang On Sloopy"/McCoys
   c. "You're the One"/Vogues

3. They're *your fire at your desire.*
   a. "Venus"/Shocking Blue
   b. "Matchbox"/Beatles
   c. "Jumpin' Jack Flash"/Rolling Stones

4. They're riding on this, *trying to catch up to you.*
   a. "Catch a Wave"/Jan and Dean
   b. "Proud Mary"/Creedence Clearwater Revival
   c. "On a Carousel"/Hollies

5. He's *swimming in a circle* and he feels he's *going down.*
   a. "No No Song"/Ringo Starr
   b. "Show Me the Way"/Peter Frampton
   c. "Stand Tall"/Burton Cummings

6. They see a time when *there'll be peace and good, and brotherhood.*
   a. "Crystal Blue Persuasion"/Tommy James and the Shondells

   b.   "People Got to Be Free"/Rascals

   c.   "Get Together"/Youngbloods

7.   He wants you to *take this badge off of* him because he *can't use it anymore.*

   a.   "I Shot the Sheriff"/Eric Clapton

   b.   "Dream Weaver"/Gary Wright

   c.   "Knockin' on Heaven's Door"/Bob Dylan

8.   *The willow turns his back on inclement weather.*

   a.   "With a Little Luck"/Wings

   b.   "Dust in the Wind"/Kansas

   c.   "You're Only Lonely"/J. D. Souther

9.   She says you're a *real tough cookie with a long history of breaking little hearts.*

   a.   "Heart of Glass"/Blondie

   b.   "Two of Hearts"/Stacey Q

   c.   "Hit Me With Your Best Shot"/Pat Benatar

10.   It's traveling *down around the corner, half a mile from here.*

   a.   "Fox on the Run"/Sweet

   b.   "Jet"/Paul McCartney

   c.   "Long Train Runnin'"/Doobie Brothers

11.   They *won't be back 'til fall;* and if they find a new girl, they *won't be back at all.*

   a.   "Time Is on My Side"/Rolling Stones

   b.   "Tired of Waiting for You"/Kinks

   c.   "C. C. Rider"/Mitch Ryder and the Detroit Wheels

12.   They wonder *who's going to tell you when it's too late* and that *things aren't so great.*

   a.   "If You Leave Me Now"/Chicago

   b.   "Drive"/Cars

   c.   "You're My Best Friend"/Queen

13.   If she would have them back, they *would never make her sad.*

   a. "If I Fell"/Beatles
   b. "Cherish"/Association
   c. "Heart Full of Soul"/Yardbirds

14. He wants her to *drop on out to spread the news.*
   a. "Rock On"/David Essex
   b. "Rock and Roll Hoochie Koo"/Rick Derringer
   c. "Island Girl"/Elton John

15. They *may not have a lot to give,* but *what* they've *got* they'll *give to you.*
   a. "Gimmie Gimmie Good Lovin'"/Crazy Elephant
   b. "Then You Can Tell Me Goodbye"/Casinos
   c. "Can't Buy Me Love"/Beatles

16. They always care and are always there *when you need satisfaction guaranteed.*
   a. "Imaginary Lover"/Atlanta Rhythm Section
   b. "Promises"/Eric Clapton
   c. "Ebony Eyes"/Bob Welch

17. You think he's *cute, a little bit shy* but he says he's *not that kind of guy.*
   a. "I Was Made for Dancin'"/Leif Garrett
   b. "Bad Case of Loving You"/Robert Palmer
   c. "Da Ya Think I'm Sexy?"/Rod Stewart

18. He's *no longer riding on the merry-go-round* because he *just had to let it go.*
   a. "Take It Away"/Paul McCartney
   b. "Watching the Wheels"/John Lennon
   c. "All Those Years Ago"/George Harrison

19. Come *take* their *hand* and *walk this land* together with them.
   a. "Sunshine of Your Love"/Cream
   b. "In-A-Gadda-Da-Vida"/Iron Butterfly
   c. "Day Tripper"/Beatles

20. They wonder *when you were young, did you question all the answers* and *envy all the dancers who had the nerve.*
    a. "Heat of the Moment"/Asia
    b. "The Heart of Rock and Roll"/Huey Lewis and the News
    c. "Wasted on the Way"/Crosby, Stills and Nash

21. They say you can *make a grown man cry.*
    a. "Start Me Up"/Rolling Stones
    b. "Sweet Talkin' Woman"/Electric Light Orchestra
    c. "Money Honey"/Bay City Rollers

22. According to them, *all the good things in life* have already been taken.
    a. "Good Thing"/Paul Revere and the Raiders
    b. "It's My Life"/Animals
    c. "The River Is Wide"/Grass Roots

23. He wants to know if he can *have one more with you.*
    a. "American Pie"/Dan McLean
    b. "Photograph"/Ringo Starr
    c. "Moondance"/Van Morrison

24. *Everybody's got to fight to be free.*
    a. "Shame on the Moon"/Bob Seger and the Silver Bullet Band
    b. "The Best of Times"/Styx
    c. "Refugee"/Tom Petty and the Heartbreakers

25. You *better get yourself together* and *join the human race.*
    a. "Sunshine Superman"/Donovan
    b. "You're So Vain"/Carly Simon
    c. "Instant Karma (We All Shine On)"/John Lennon

26. They claim to be *a lovable man who can take you to the nearest star.*
    a. "Vehicle"/Ides of March

    b. "Come On Up"/Young Rascals

    c. "Back Door Man"/Doors

27. He wants the *long-distance operator* to help him *get in touch with Marie.*

    a. "(Marie's the Name of) His Latest Flame"/Elvis Presley

    b. "Memphis"/Johnny Rivers

    c. "Operator"/Jim Croce

28. They *had such happiness together,* but *it's sad to see it's gone forever.*

    a. "Then You Can Tell Me Goodbye"/Casinos

    b. "Yesterday's Gone"/Chad and Jeremy

    c. "You've Got to Hide Your Love Away"/Beatles

29. They stood *high upon a mountaintop, naked to the world, in front of every kind of girl.*

    a. "Get Off My Cloud"/Rolling Stones

    b. "Spill the Wine"/Eric Burdon and War

    c. "Eight Miles High"/Byrds

30. *Disappointment* used to *haunt* their *dreams.*

    a. "Stormy"/Classics IV

    b. "I'm a Believer"/Monkees

    c. "I Feel Fine"/Beatles

31. The first kick he took was when he *hit the ground.*

    a. "Never Surrender"/Corey Hart

    b. "Born in the U.S.A."/Bruce Springsteen

    c. "Keeping the Faith"/Billy Joel

32. *When you cast your spell and hypnotize with those eyes,* you'll get your way.

    a. "Take My Breath Away"/Berlin

    b. "Magic"/Cars

    c. "You Can Do Magic"/America

33. They claim that *other guys are trying to break* them *up and pull* them *apart.*

    a. "I Think We're Alone Now"/Tommy James and the Shondells

    b. "She'd Rather Be With Me"/Turtles

    c. "Can't You See That She's Mine"/Dave Clark Five

34. After *strong words in the staff room,* the *accusations fly.*

    a. "Don't Stand So Close to Me"/Police

    b. "Do You Really Want to Hurt Me"/Culture Club

    c. "Is There Something I Should Know"/Duran Duran

35. They *ran into a great big hassle* down in El Paso.

    a. "I Thank You"/ZZ Top

    b. "Saturday Night Special"/Lynyrd Skynyrd

    c. "Take the Money and Run"/Steve Miller Band

36. *Night is calling* and they *are falling.*

    a. "Hot Blooded"/Foreigner

    b. "One on One"/Daryl Hall and John Oates

    c. "Dance With Me"/Orleans

37. They *know the neighborhood* and that *talk is cheap when the story is good.*

    a. "Take It on the Run"/REO Speedwagon

    b. "Don't Do Me Like That"/Tom Petty and the Heartbreakers

    c. "Slow Ride"/Foghat

38. You can *spend all your time making love* or *you can spend all your love making time.*

    a. "Life's Been Good"/Joe Walsh

    b. "A Little Bit More"/Dr. Hook

    c. "Take It to the Limit"/Eagles

39. *Thunder only happens when it's raining.*

    a. "Sky High"/Jigsaw

    b. "Fernando"/Abba

    c. "Dreams"/Fleetwood Mac

40. She doesn't *remember Aretha Franklin, the queen of soul.*
   a. "Rock 'n' Roll Fantasy"/Bad Company
   b. "Hey Nineteen"/Steely Dan
   c. "Shannon"/Henry Gross

41. They can *jump in the river and stay drunk all the time.*
   a. "Bottle of Wine"/Fireballs
   b. "Going Up the Country"/Canned Heat
   c. "Sweet Cherry Wine"/Tommy James and the Shondells

42. They claim that the *women are frustrated* because *they have to be in by 12:00.*
   a. "In the Midnight Hour"/Young Rascals
   b. "Dirty Water"/Standells
   c. "Will You Be Staying After Sunday"/Peppermint Rainbow

43. They feel that nothing they do *don't seem to work; it only seems to make matters worse.*
   a. "Nineteenth Nervous Breakdown"/Rolling Stones
   b. "Needles and Pins"/Searchers
   c. "I Don't Want to Spoil the Party"/Beatles

44. They *never understood a single word he said, but helped him drink his wine.*
   a. "Rain Dance"/Guess Who
   b. "Mighty Quinn (Quinn the Eskimo)"/Manfred Mann
   c. "Joy to the World"/Three Dog Night

45. You *don't need a weatherman to know which way the wind blows.*
   a. "Catch the Wind"/Donovan
   b. "Subterranean Homesick Blues"/Bob Dylan
   c. "Windy"/Association

46. Even though they've got a wife now, when they make love they *still see your face.*
   a. "How Much I Feel"/Ambrosia
   b. "Walking on a Thin Line"/Huey Lewis and the News
   c. "Kiss You All Over"/Exile

47. They rode upon the *mystery ship* and *sailed into history.*
   a. "Beginnings"/Chicago
   b. "The Crystal Ship"/Doors
   c. "Ride Captain Ride"/Blues Image

48. He's *just tired and bored* with himself knowing that *you can't start a fire without a spark.*
   a. "Dancing in the Dark"/Bruce Springsteen
   b. "Missing You"/John Waite
   c. "Big Log"/Robert Plant

49. He wonders whether *Major Tom* can still hear him.
   a. "We Don't Talk Anymore"/Cliff Richard
   b. "Uncle Albert/Admiral Halsey"/Paul McCartney
   c. "Space Oddity"/David Bowie

50. *She just can't be chained to a life where nothing's gained,* though *nothing's lost.*
   a. "Na Na Hey Hey Kiss Him Goodbye"/Steam
   b. "Green-Eyed Lady"/Sugarloaf
   c. "Ruby Tuesday"/Rolling Stones

51. They see *sidewalk scenes and black limousines.*
   a. "Eight Miles High"/Byrds
   b. "People Are Strange"/Doors
   c. "Nights in White Satin"/Moody Blues

52. *Everybody's talking* about him and *walking like* him.
   a. "New Kid in Town"/Eagles
   b. "Hot Rod Hearts"/Robbie Dupree
   c. "Dirty White Boy"/Foreigner

53. They want you to do it *good* by putting it *into shape.*
    a. "Whip It"/Devo
    b. "Shake It Up"/Cars
    c. "Real Love"/Doobie Brothers

54. It seems to them that *we've got to solve our problems individually.*
    a. "You've Got Your Troubles"/Fortunes
    b. "Problems Problems"/Everly Brothers
    c. "People Got to Be Free"/Rascals

55. After Holly *hitchhiked across the U.S.A.* and *plucked her eyes* and *shaved her legs* on the way, *he was a she.*
    a. "Young Americans"/David Bowie
    b. "Walk This Way"/Aerosmith
    c. "Walk on the Wild Side"/Lou Reed

56. Although they don't have one dollar to spend, they wonder *how much do* they *really need?"*
    a. "I Got You Babe"/Sonny and Cher
    b. "Daydream Believer"/Monkees
    c. "Can't Buy Me Love"/Beatles

57. She makes them *feel so good*; and she makes them *feel all right.*
    a. "Fever"/McCoys
    b. "Glad All Over"/Dave Clark Five
    c. "Gloria"/Shadows of Knight

58. Planning their cross-country safari, they *can't wait for June.*
    a. "Surfin' U.S.A."/Beach Boys
    b. "In the Summertime"/Mungo Jerry
    c. "Surf City"/Jan and Dean

59. Although they got their hands on a dollar bill, *the dollar bill flew away.*
    a. "Won't Get Fooled Again"/Who
    b. "Acapulco Gold"/Rainy Daze

    c. "I Just Want to Celebrate"/Rare Earth

60. *Summertime will be a love-in there.*
    a. "Last Plane to London"/Rose Garden
    b. "San Francisco (Be Sure To Wear Flowers in Your Hair)"/Scott McKenzie
    c. "Monterey"/Animals

61. *After nine days,* they realized that *the desert had turned to sea.*
    a. "Smoke on the Water"/Deep Purple
    b. "Shambala"/Three Dog Night
    c. "A Horse With No Name"/America

62. *Whatever will be will be* but *the future is* theirs *to see.*
    a. "Baby Hold On"/Eddie Money
    b. "This Time"/John Cougar
    c. "I Want You to Want Me"/Cheap Trick

63. *After all the years,* they say you can still *scratch* their *itch.*
    a. "Still the One"/Orleans
    b. "Feels Like the First Time"/Foreigner
    c. "You Make Loving Fun"/Fleetwood Mac

64. Although she's been gone for some time, they promise to *meet* her *all the way.*
    a. "Rosanna"/Toto
    b. "Open Arms"/Journey
    c. "Here I Am"/Air Supply

65. *Time keeps on slipping into the future.*
    a. "What Is Life"/George Harrison
    b. "You'll Accomp'ny Me"/Bob Seger
    c. "Fly Like an Eagle"/Steve Miller Band

66. They want you to know *when you're gonna give* them *some time* and when you'll make their *motor run.*
    a. "My Best Friend's Girl"/Cars
    b. "My Sharona"/Knack

    c. "We Got the Beat"/Go-Go's

67. You've got *the greatest thing since rock and roll.*

    a. "You Baby"/Turtles

    b. "Do You Believe in Magic"/Lovin' Spoonful

    c. "Denise"/Randy and the Rainbows

68. If they left here tomorrow, they wonder whether you'd *still remember* them.

    a. "The Best of Times"/Styx

    b. "Free Bird"/Lynyrd Skynyrd

    c. "Take Me in Your Arms"/Doobie Brothers

69. She stood in the street *smiling from her head to her feet.*

    a. "Do Wah Diddy Diddy"/Manfred Mann

    b. "All Right Now"/Free

    c. "I'm a Believer"/Monkees

70. They *will get by*; they *will survive.*

    a. "Manic Monday"/Bangles

    b. "Livin' on a Prayer"/Bon Jovi

    c. "Touch of Grey"/Grateful Dead

71. He claims she led him *away from home just to keep him from being alone.*

    a. "Maggie May"/Rod Stewart

    b. "Cracklin' Rosie"/Neil Diamond

    c. "Brown-Eyed Girl"/Van Morrison

72. *Living without you is driving* them *crazy.*

    a. "Wild Thing"/Troggs

    b. "I Need You"/Beatles

    c. "Cry Like a Baby"/Boxtops

73. They say that they're *wrong to keep* doing this.

    a. "(I've Been) Searchin' So Long"/Chicago

    b. "Holdin' On to Yesterday"/Ambrosia

    c. "Smokin' in the Boy's Room"/Brownsville Station

74. A *cop* finally *broke* their *bottle* of this.

    a. "Love Potion Number Nine"/Searchers
    b. "Bottle of Wine"/Fireballs
    c. "Dirty Water"/Standells

75. *At this moment, you mean everything* to them.
    a. "Caught Up in You"/38 Special
    b. "Vacation"/Go-Go's
    c. "Come On Eileen"/Dexys Midnight Runners

76. They've *forgotten what* they're *fighting for.*
    a. "Everybody Wants to Rule the World"/Tears for Fears
    b. "Owner of a Lonely Heart"/Yes
    c. "Can't Fight This Feeling"/REO Speedwagon

77. They *know that people will find a way to go* and that their *love will grow for all* they *know.*
    a. "Count on Me"/Jefferson Starship
    b. "Listen to What the Man Said"/Wings
    c. "Say You Love Me"/Fleetwood Mac

78. You *hold* them *tight, really know how to dance* and *always whisper in* their *ear things* they *like to hear.*
    a. "Imaginary Lover"/Atlanta Rhythm Section
    b. "Good Girls Don't"/Knack
    c. "What I Like About You"/Romantics

79. She *knows how to use them.*
    a. "The Boys of Summer"/Don Henley
    b. "Rich Girl"/Darryl Hall and John Oates
    c. "Legs"/ZZ Top

80. *Nothing can cool* him *but* he's *feeling fine.*
    a. "Fire"/Jimi Hendrix
    b. "Burning Love"/Elvis Presley
    c. "Great Balls of Fire"/Jerry Lee Lewis

81. Even though their *love holds on,* he adds that *you'd be better off alone.*
    a. "Oh Sherrie"/Steve Perry

    b. "Against All Odds"/Phil Collins

    c. "You Belong to the City"/Glenn Fry

82. He can't tell you that he's something's he's not no matter how hard he tries, because he just *won't ever be able to give you something* he *just* hasn't *got.*

    a. "Into the Night"/Benny Mardones

    b. "Two Out of Three Ain't Bad"/Meat Loaf

    c. "Cuts Like a Knife"/Bryan Adams

83. They say that eventually *it will come back to you.*

    a. "Give Peace a Chance"/Plastic Ono Band

    b. "Reminiscing"/Little River Band

    c. "Peg"/Steely Dan

84. The lady who *made* them *nervous also gave* them *breakfast.*

    a. "Wrapped Around Your Finger"/Police

    b. "Lady"/Little River Band

    c. "Down Under"/Men at Work

85. They wonder if you're *happy* and *satisfied* now that they're gone, and *how long you can stand the heat.*

    a. "Another One Bites the Dust"/Queen

    b. "Whatcha Gonna Do?"/Pablo Cruise

    c. "Who's Crying Now"/Journey

86. They say that because *you never take advice* and *you're willing to sacrifice* their love, *someday you'll pay the price.*

    a. "Find Another Fool"/Quarterflash

    b. "We're Not Gonna Take It"/Twisted Sister

    c. "Cold As Ice"/Foreigner

87. He'll never forget *the way you look tonight.*

    a. "Tonight's the Night"/Rod Stewart

    b. "Missing You"/John Waite

    c. "The Lady in Red"/Chris DeBurgh

88. *Too many hearts are falling in the river.*

   a. "The Things We Do for Love"/10cc

   b. "It's Sad to Belong"/England Dan and John Ford Coley

   c. "Winners and Losers"/Hamilton, Joe Frank and Reynolds

89. He has *such a supple wrist.*

   a. "Pinball Wizard"/Who

   b. "The Boy From New York City"/Ad Libs

   c. "Honky Cat"/Elton John

90. It's going to take *a whole lot of spending money* as well as *time and patience* to do it right.

   a. "Money for Nothing"/Dire Straits

   b. "Invisible Touch"/Genesis

   c. "Got My Mind Set on You"/George Harrison

91. They've got *quivers down* their *backbone* and *shivers in* their *knee bone.*

   a. "Hippy Hippy Shake"/Swinging Blue Jeans

   b. "Fever"/McCoys

   c. "Shakin' All Over"/Guess Who

92. *This land's the place* they *love,* and *here* they always will *stay.*

   a. "Massachusetts"/Bee Gees

   b. "Ferry Cross the Mersey"/Gerry and the Pacemakers

   c. "San Franciscan Nights"/Animals

93. They describe you as *silk and satin, leather and lace; black panties with an angel's face.*

   a. "Leather and Lace"/Stevie Nicks with Don Henley

   b. "Ebony and Ivory"/Paul McCartney and Stevie Wonder

   c. "Abracadabra"/Steve Miller Band

94. *Hail! Hail! Rock 'n' Roll!*

   a. "Rock and Roll Is Here to Stay"/Danny and the Juniors

   b. "School Day"/Chuck Berry
   c. "Those Oldies but Goodies"/Little Caesar and the Romans

95. They'll be with you *when the stars start falling.*
   a. "For Your Love"/Yardbirds
   b. "Sunshine of Your Love"/Cream
   c. "You Keep Me Hangin' On"/Vanilla Fudge

96. They're *just a poor boy* and *nobody loves* them.
   a. "Love Is the Drug"/Roxy Music
   b. "Imaginary Lover"/Atlanta Rhythm Section
   c. "Bohemian Rhapsody"/Queen

97. They're going to love you *'til the heavens stop the rain.*
   a. "Then You Can Tell Me Goodbye"/Casinos
   b. "Touch Me"/Doors
   c. "Cara Mia"/Jay and the Americans

98. You'd *be* his *breath should* he *grow old.*
   a. "Against All Odds"/Phil Collins
   b. "You're in My Heart"/Rod Stewart
   c. "Wonderful Tonight"/Eric Clapton

99. Because there's *an interstate running through* his *front yard,* he says *ain't that America.*
   a. "My Hometown"/Bruce Springsteen
   b. "Pink Houses"/John Cougar Mellencamp
   c. "Straight From the Heart"/Bryan Adams

100. They know that *what the winner doesn't know, a gambler understands.*
   a. "Ramblin' Gamblin' Man"/Bob Seger System
   b. "Straight On"/Heart
   c. "Take It to the Limit"/Eagles

We Don't Need No Education
LEVEL THREE

1. It's *too big to hide and it can't be denied.*
   a. "Soul Deep"/Boxtops
   b. "My Baby Loves Lovin'"/White Plains
   c. "People Got to Be Free"/Rascals

2. He's been *sitting for so long* wasting time *staring at the phone.*
   a. "One More Night"/Phil Collins
   b. "Break My Stride"/Matthew Wilder
   c. "I'm Still Standing"/Elton John

3. He wants you to *turn* him *loose.*
   a. "Footloose"/Kenny Loggins
   b. "Authority Song"/John Cougar Mellencamp
   c. "Turn Me Loose"/Loverboy

4. *Somebody's going to hurt someone before the night is through.*
   a. "Heartache Tonight"/Eagles
   b. "What a Fool Believes"/Doobie Brothers
   c. "When You're in Love With a Beautiful Woman"/Dr. Hook

5. Last night they *met a new girl in the neighborhood.*
   a. "Do You Want to Know a Secret"/Beatles
   b. "I'm Into Something Good"/Herman's Hermits
   c. "New Girl in School"/Jan and Dean

6. They *really love your peaches* and want *to shake your tree.*
   a. "Hooked on a Feeling"/Blue Swede

  b. "The Joker"/Steve Miller Band

  c. "You Ain't Seen Nothing Yet"/Bachman-Turner Overdrive

 7. *The past is just a goodbye.*

  a. "Hurdy Gurdy Man"/Donovan

  b. "For What It's Worth"/Buffalo Springfield

  c. "Teach Your Children"/Crosby, Stills, Nash and Young

 8. With *two hearts born to run,* they wonder *who'll be the lonely one.*

  a. "Heartache Tonight"/Eagles

  b. "Lonely People"/America

  c. "Who's Crying Now"/Journey

 9. The *six-gun sound* is their *claim to fame.*

  a. "Bad Company"/Bad Company

  b. "Saturday Night Special"/Lynyrd Skynyrd

  c. "Live and Let Die"/Wings

 10. They know *how to whisper and cry and find the answers and how to lie.*

  a. "I'm Not in Love"/10cc

  b. "Making Love out of Nothing At All"/Air Supply

  c. "Don't Stand So Close to Me"/Police

 11. *No one told* them *about her, though they all knew.*

  a. "Day Tripper"/Beatles

  b. "She's Not There"/Zombies

  c. "Susan"/Buckinghams

 12. *Smile on your brother.*

  a. "Reach Out of the Darkness"/Friend and Lover

  b. "The Beat Goes On"/Sonny and Cher

  c. "Get Together"/Youngbloods

 13. You don't need this *to help you face the world each day.*

  a. "Kicks"/Paul Revere and the Raiders

    b. "Mother's Little Helper"/Rolling Stones
    c. "White Rabbit"/Jefferson Airplane

14. Their car *ain't got a back seat or a rear window* but it sure *gets* them *where* they *want to go.*
    a. "Surf City"/Jan and Dean
    b. "Little Deuce Coupe"/Beach Boys
    c. "Bucket-T"/Ronny and the Daytonas

15. They claim that *when* they *first met you, you didn't have no shoes, and now you're walking around like you're front-page news.*
    a. "Let Me Be"/Turtles
    b. "Where Were You When I Needed You"/Grass Roots
    c. "(I'm Not Your) Steppin' Stone"/Monkees

16. Because he's *high on cocaine*, they say he'd *better watch* his *speed.*
    a. "Casey Jones"/Grateful Dead
    b. "Sky Pilot"/Eric Burdon and the Animals
    c. "Jet Airliner"/Steve Miller Band

17. They *can't wait forever to know if you'll be true.*
    a. "I've Been Lonely Too Long"/Young Rascals
    b. "Time Won't Let Me"/Outsiders
    c. "Tired of Waiting for You"/Kinks

18. They *don't have time to take a fast train.*
    a. "Time Is on My Side"/Rolling Stones
    b. "Eight Miles High"/Byrds
    c. "The Letter"/Boxtops

19. They've got parts *made in Japan.*
    a. "Dream Police"/Cheap Trick
    b. "Mr. Roboto"/Styx
    c. "Magic Man"/Heart

20. They see the *yellow man, brown man, white man* and *red man looking for Uncle Sam* to give them *a helping hand*, but because *everybody's kicking sand*, they see that *we're living in a plastic land.*

    a. "Y.M.C.A."/Village People
    b. "Dream On"/Aerosmith
    c. "Living in the U.S.A."/Steve Miller Band

21. You *woo* them until *the sun comes up.*

    a. "Here Comes My Girl"/Tom Petty and the Heartbreakers
    b. "Say You Love Me"/Fleetwood Mac
    c. "Afternoon Delight"/Starland Vocal Band

22. He believes it *can help* get him *through the night.*

    a. "Oh Sherrie"/Steve Perry
    b. "Dream Weaver"/Gary Wright
    c. "Mind Games"/John Lennon

23. They say *there's a reason for the warm sweet nights* and *for the candlelight.*

    a. "You're the Inspiration"/Chicago
    b. "Some Kind of Wonderful"/Grand Funk Railroad
    c. "Let Your Love Flow"/Bellamy Brothers

24. They've *come to give you a hand and lead you to the Promised Land.*

    a. "Come Sail Away"/Styx
    b. "Free Ride"/Edgar Winter Group
    c. "Black Water"/Doobie Brothers

25. They want her to *use* their *mind and* they'll be her *teacher.*

    a. "Mrs. Robinson"/Simon and Garfunkel
    b. "Wendy"/Beach Boys
    c. "Carrie-Anne"/Hollies

26. She's *a witch of trouble* who's *in love with you.*

    a. "Strange Brew"/Cream

    b. "Devil With a Blue Dress On"/Mitch Ryder
    c. "Witchy Woman"/Eagles

27. He dreamed that he *sailed away to China in a little rowboat to find you.*
    a. "Coming Up"/Paul McCartney
    b. "China Girl"/David Bowie
    c. "Break My Stride"/Matthew Wilder

28. *She won't give up because she's seventeen.*
    a. "Sweet Talkin' Woman"/Electric Light Orchestra
    b. "Let's Go"/Cars
    c. "Good Girls Don't"/Knack

29. It *takes control and slowly tears you apart.*
    a. "Sledgehammer"/Peter Gabriel
    b. "Invisible Touch"/Genesis
    c. "Freedom"/George Michael

30. He *can see the sunset* in your eyes.
    a. "Sunshine Superman"/Donovan
    b. "Baby I Love Your Way"/Peter Frampton
    c. "Doctor My Eyes"/Jackson Browne

31. Because *pictures came and broke your heart,* they say to *put the blame on VCR.*
    a. "Another One Bites the Dust"/Queen
    b. "Video Killed the Radio Star"/Buggles
    c. "FM (No Static at All)"/Steely Dan

32. When the bell rings to end the workday, *nothing else matters at all.*
    a. "Five O'Clock World"/Vogues
    b. "Dance, Dance, Dance"/Beach Boys
    c. "Baby It's You"/Smith

33. They're *coming home* to *where the skies are so blue.*
    a. "Philadelphia Freedom"/Elton John Band
    b. "Waterloo"/Abba
    c. "Sweet Home Alabama"/Lynyrd Skynyrd

34. Because *the hangman isn't hanging,* they *put you in the street.*
    a. "Point of Know Return"/Kansas
    b. "Do It Again"/Steely Dan
    c. "Still the Same"/Bob Seger and the Silver Bullet Band

35. They've realized that *the best part of love is the thinnest slice.*
    a. "Lost in Love"/Air Supply
    b. "Crazy on You"/Heart
    c. "Maybe I'm Amazed"/Wings

36. They're *looking for someone to change* their *life* and are hoping *for a miracle in* their *life.*
    a. "Question"/Moody Blues
    b. "Miracles"/Jefferson Starship
    c. "(I've Been) Searchin' So Long"/Chicago

37. They're *not looking for a love that'll last* because they *know what they need* and they *need it fast.*
    a. "Urgent"/Foreigner
    b. "Too Much Time on My Hands"/Styx
    c. "Hold Me"/Fleetwood Mac

38. They are *feeling better* because *she took* them *to her doctor and he told* them *of a cure.*
    a. "Feel Like Makin' Love"/Bad Company
    b. "You Ain't Seen Nothin' Yet"/Bachman-Turner Overdrive
    c. "Good Lovin'"/Young Rascals

39. You need this *when you're feeling low and the fish won't bite.*
    a. "A Little Bit of Soul"/Music Explosion
    b. "I Want Candy"/Strangeloves
    c. "Love Potion Number Nine"/Searchers

40. He warns you not to do it *until he gets you to the other side.*

    a. "Lay Down Sally"/Eric Clapton
    b. "Don't Pay the Ferryman"/Chris De Burgh
    c. "Show Me the Way"/Peter Frampton

41. *Here* they *come again.*
    a. "Monkees Theme"/Monkees
    b. "I Get Around"/Beach Boys
    c. "Catch Us If You Can"/Dave Clark Five

42. If he *listened long enough to you,* he'd *find a way* to think *that it's all true.*
    a. "Your Song"/Elton John
    b. "Never Gonna Fall in Love Again"/Eric Carmen
    c. "Reason to Believe"/Rod Stewart

43. They *think you're wild when you flash that fragile smile.*
    a. "Wrapped Around Your Finger"/Police
    b. "You Might Think"/Cars
    c. "(Keep Feeling) Fascination"/Human League

44. A *circumstance beyond* their *control* got into the house *like a pigeon from hell.*
    a. "Back on the Chain Gang"/Pretenders
    b. "Here Comes the Rain Again"/Eurythmics
    c. "Tainted Love"/Soft Cell

45. Loving you *isn't the right thing to do.*
    a. "Go Your Own Way"/Fleetwood Mac
    b. "Lyin' Eyes"/Eagles
    c. "Run Joey Run"/David Geddes

46. He doesn't *want your money* and tells you to *save it for a rainy day.*
    a. "Fire"/Jimi Hendrix
    b. "We Gotta Get You a Woman"/Todd Rundgren
    c. "Give Me Love (Give Me Peace on Earth)"/George Harrison

47. They wonder whether they didn't *see you crying.*

    a. "Amanda"/Boston
    b. "Emotional Rescue"/Rolling Stones
    c. "I Want You to Want Me"/Cheap Trick

48. When you're here, *you see the darnedest things.*
    a. "Africa"/Toto
    b. "Middle of the Road"/Pretenders
    c. "Electric Avenue"/Eddy Grant

49. *Sweet devotion is not for* them.
    a. "We Are the Champions"/Queen
    b. "Hot Blooded"/Foreigner
    c. "Goodbye Stranger"/Supertramp

50. Ever since he was *a kid in school,* he *messed around with all the rules.*
    a. "I Was Only Joking"/Rod Stewart
    b. "I'm Alright"/Kenny Loggins
    c. "This Time"/John Cougar

51. Because *another kiss is all you need,* he knows that *you're gonna have to face it.*
    a. "Addicted to Love"/Robert Palmer
    b. "Your Love Is Driving Me Crazy"/Sammy Hagar
    c. "No More Lonely Nights"/Paul McCartney

52. Although people have *a name for the winners in the world,* they *want a name when* they *lose.*
    a. "Lost Without Your Love"/Bread
    b. "Baby Come Back"/Player
    c. "Deacon Blues"/Steely Dan

53. She sends this when they *get lonely* and they're *sure* they've *had enough.*
    a. "Miracles"/Jefferson Starship
    b. "The Air That I Breathe"/Hollies
    c. "Radar Love"/Golden Earring

54. Their girlfriend tells them that *everything will turn out alright.*

    a. "I Should Have Known Better"/Beatles
    b. "Spooky"/Classics IV
    c. "Don't Worry Baby"/Beach Boys

55. They ask the *Mississippi moon to keep on shining* on them.
    a. "Freebird"/Lynyrd Skynyrd
    b. "Black Water"/Doobie Brothers
    c. "Peaceful Easy Feeling"/Eagles

56. *She only comes out at night.*
    a. "Hungry Like the Wolf"/Duran Duran
    b. "Maneater"/Daryl Hall and John Oates
    c. "Uptown Girl"/Billy Joel

57. *Paranoia strikes deep; into your life it will creep.*
    a. "Turn! Turn! Turn!"/Byrds
    b. "Suspicion"/Terry Stafford
    c. "For What It's Worth"/Buffalo Springfield

58. *You should have heard her just around midnight.*
    a. "Gloria"/Them
    b. "Young Girl"/Gary Puckett and the Union Gap
    c. "Brown Sugar"/Rolling Stones

59. Though *you can't see the morning,* they *can see the light.*
    a. "Born to Wander"/Rare Earth
    b. "Let It Ride"/Bachman-Turner Overdrive
    c. "American Woman"/Guess Who

60. He *used to be a rolling stone if the cause was right.*
    a. "Rebel Yell"/Billy Idol
    b. "Philadelphia Freedom"/Elton John Band
    c. "Fame"/David Bowie

61. They say that *it's a terrible thing to lose.*
    a. "Somebody to Love"/Queen
    b. "Livin' Thing"/Electric Light Orchestra
    c. "Jet Airliner"/Steve Miller Band

62. They sometimes find themselves *alone and regretting some foolish thing, some little thing* they've *done.*

   a. "We Can Work It Out"/Beatles
   b. "A Little Bit Me, a Little Bit You"/Monkees
   c. "Don't Let Me Be Misunderstood"/Animals

63. They advise you not to *lose your grip on the dreams of the past* because *you must fight just to keep them alive.*

   a. "Do You Believe in Love"/Huey Lewis and the News
   b. "Eye of the Tiger"/Survivor
   c. "Up Where We Belong"/Joe Cocker and Jennifer Warnes

64. They *want to tear your world apart.*

   a. "De Do Do Do, De Da Da Da"/Police
   b. "Doo Doo Doo Doo Doo"/Rolling Stones
   c. "Do Ya"/Electric Light Orchestra

65. He's *just gonna walk up to her* and *gonna talk to her tonight.*

   a. "(You're) Having My Baby"/Paul Anka
   b. "Baby, I Love Your Way"/Peter Frampton
   c. "Somebody's Baby"/Jackson Browne

66. He says *you've got a lot of nerve to say you are* his *friend.*

   a. "Positively 4th Street"/Bob Dylan
   b. "Alone Again, Naturally"/Gilbert O'Sullivan
   c. "Solitary Man"/Neil Diamond

67. They *ain't got no time for lovin'* because their *time is all used up.*

   a. "I'm a Man"/Spencer Davis Group
   b. "Ramblin' Man"/Allman Brothers Band
   c. "No Time"/Guess Who

68. When they walked into the room, *there was voodoo* in the air, from which they became *captured by your style.*

   a. "Magic Man"/Heart

   b. "Evil Woman"/Electric Light Orchestra

   c. "So in to You"/Atlanta Rhythm Section

69. The *full moon is calling, the fever is high,* and the *wicked wind whispers and moans.*

   a. "I'd Really Love to See You Tonight"/England Dan and John Ford Coley

   b. "Moonlight Feels Right"/Starbuck

   c. "One of These Nights"/Eagles

70. They say *there's nothing wrong with* their *state of mental heath.*

   a. "Take Me to Heart"/Quarterflash

   b. "Vacation"/Go-Go's

   c. "Who Can It Be Now?"/Men at Work

71. *Butterflies are free to fly away.*

   a. "Someone Saved My Life Tonight"/Elton John

   b. "She's Gone"/Daryl Hall and John Oates

   c. "Free Bird"/Lynyrd Skynyrd

72. *When the sun comes up,* they'll *be on top,* and *you'll be down there looking up.*

   a. "Don't Bring Me Down"/Animals

   b. "96 Tears"/? and the Mysterians

   c. "Here Comes the Sun"/Beatles

73. *They cry in the dark so you can't see their tears.*

   a. "Hell Is for Children"/Pat Benatar

   b. "Only the Lonely"/Motels

   c. "Alone"/Heart

74. He was *living to run and running to live.*

   a. "Turn Me Loose"/Loverboy

   b. "Against the Wind"/Bob Seger

    c. "Hungry Heart"/Bruce Springsteen

75. They wonder *does she walk, does she talk, does she come complete.*

    a. "Centerfold"/J. Geils Band

    b. "I Ran (So Far Away)"/Flock of Seagulls

    c. "Talking in Your Sleep"/Romantics

76. *Nothing's the matter with your head,* so they tell you to *come and find it* and *get it together.*

    a. "Bang a Gong (Get It On)"/T. Rex

    b. "Come and Get Your Love"/Redbone

    c. "Some Kind of Wonderful"/Grand Funk

77. You *could never look* them *in the eye.*

    a. "Stop Draggin' My Heart Around"/Stevie Nicks and Tom Petty

    b. "Private Eyes"/Darryl Hall and John Oates

    c. "Tell It Like It Is"/Heart

78. *There's a little black spot on the sun today.*

    a. "King of Pain"/Police

    b. "Space Oddity"/David Bowie

    c. "Love Is Like Oxygen"/Sweet

79. This is the period when *love runs high.*

    a. "This Magic Moment"/Jay and the Americans

    b. "All Day and All of the Night"/Kinks

    c. "Time of the Season"/Zombies

80. If you take them *to a disco,* you'll never even get them *out on the floor.*

    a. "I Love Rock 'N Roll"/Joan Jett and the Blackhearts

    b. "Shake It Up"/Cars

    c. "Old Time Rock and Roll"/Bob Seger and the Silver Bullet Band

81. *Save your crying for the day.*

    a. "Don't Cry"/Asia

    b. "Stand Tall"/Burton Cummings

    c. "Fool (If You Think It's Over)"/Chris Rea

82. His *bed is* here and *that's good enough* for him.

    a. "Born in the U.S.A."/Bruce Springsteen

    b. "Small Town"/John Cougar Mellencamp

    c. "Allentown"/Billy Joel

83. They *saw Betty Lou* and *danced with Peggy Sue,* but they *knew they wouldn't do.*

    a. "You Baby"/Turtles

    b. "Barbara Ann"/Regents

    c. "I Like It Like That"/Dave Clark Five

84. For them, it *feels so right being with you here tonight.*

    a. "Good Thing"/Paul Revere and the Raiders

    b. "Go All the Way"/Raspberries

    c. "I Feel Fine"/Beatles

85. They *wanted a woman* but *never bargained for you.*

    a. "Dazed and Confused"/Led Zeppelin

    b. "Hand Me Down World"/Guess Who

    c. "Let It Ride"/Bachman-Turner Overdrive

86. *If the real thing doesn't do the trick,* they say you'd *better make up something quick* or else *you're gonna burn to the wick.*

    a. "I'm on Fire"/Dwight Tilley Band

    b. "Barracuda"/Heart

    c. "One Way or Another"/Blondie

87. *The dream is over.*

    a. "God"/John Lennon

    b. "An American Dream"/Dirt Band

    c. "Dreams"/Fleetwood Mac

88. It seems he's *got to have a change of scene* because every night he has *the strangest dream.*

    a. "School's Out"/Alice Cooper

    b. "Rocket Man"/Elton John

    c. "Feeling Alright"/Joe Cocker

89. Although *he's been a good friend,* lately *something's changed* and *it ain't hard to define.*
    a. "Without Your Love"/Roger Daltrey
    b. "Steal Away"/Robbie Dupree
    c. "Jessie's Girl"/Rick Springfield

90. They concede that *wearing skin-tight pants, you look like a girl.*
    a. "Are You a Boy or Are You a Girl?"/Barbarians
    b. "How Do You Do It?"/Gerry and the Pacemakers
    c. "Walk Like a Man"/Four Seasons

91. They feel you *don't try very hard to please* them, and with *what you know it should be easy.*
    a. "Easy to Be Hard"/Three Dog Night
    b. "Do You Love Me"/Contours
    c. "The Last Time"/Rolling Stones

92. *Over at Johnny's place, a chick got up and slapped Johnny's face.*
    a. "Third Time Lucky"/Foghat
    b. "Another One Bites the Dust"/Queen
    c. "The Boys Are Back in Town"/Thin Lizzy

93. There was *a small-town girl living in a lonely world* who took a train *going anywhere.*
    a. "Shadows of the Night"/Pat Benatar
    b. "Don't Stop Believin'"/Journey
    c. "Jack and Diane"/John Cougar

94. They say that *some girls like to handle everything they see.*
    a. "California Girls"/Beach Boys
    b. "She'd Rather Be With Me"/Turtles
    c. "Under My Thumb"/Rolling Stones

95. It's *always the same* and *it's just a shame.*
    a. "Round and Round"/Ratt

    b. "You Might Think"/Cars

    c. "That's All!"/Genesis

96. Though you gave a promise to them, *you broke it.*

    a. "These Eyes"/Guess Who

    b. "Indian Giver"/1910 Fruitgum Company

    c. "Lies"/Knickerbockers

97. She's got *lovin' like quicksand.*

    a. "Hush"/Deep Purple

    b. "You Keep Me Hangin' On"/Vanilla Fudge

    c. "Cinnamon"/Derek

98. *As a cloud appears above your head* and *is moving nearer still, Aurora Borealis comes into view.*

    a. "Sweet Dreams"/Air Supply

    b. "Freeze-Frame"/J. Geils Band

    c. "I Ran (So Far Away)"/A Flock of Seagulls

99. As you and they *would scream together songs unsung,* this is what *shone in your eyes* and was *telling* them *what* their *heart meant.*

    a. "Heat of the Moment"/Asia

    b. "Real Love"/Doobie Brothers

    c. "Body Language"/Queen

100. They see *Johnny* coming, *singing oldies, goldies* such as *"Be Bop a Lula"* and *"I Got a Woman."*

    a. "Hip to Be Square"/Huey Lewis and the News

    b. "Walk of Life"/Dire Straits

    c. "Rock the Casbah"/Clash

Take It to the Limit
LEVEL FOUR

1. *We can build another day.*
   a. "Dream Weaver"/Gary Wright
   b. "Philadelphia Freedom"/Elton John Band
   c. "The Love That's Deep Within You"/Moody Blues

2. They were *feeling kinda seasick as the crowd called out for more.*
   a. "A Whiter Shade of Pale"/Procol Harum
   b. "Travelin' Band"/Creedence Clearwater Revival
   c. "Sloop John B"/Beach Boys

3. They're *walking hand in hand across the bridge at midnight.*
   a. "Lawyers in Love"/Jackson Browne
   b. "Hot Girls in Love"/Loverboy
   c. "Girls on Film"/Duran Duran

4. They've got *two cats in the yard.*
   a. "No Milk Today"/Herman's Hermits
   b. "Our House"/Crosby, Stills, Nash and Young
   c. "Different Drum"/Stone Poneys

5. If people stare, *just let them burn their eyes on you moving.*
   a. "Hold Your Head Up"/Argent
   b. "Bang a Gong (Get It On)"/T. Rex
   c. "Golden Years"/David Bowie

6. They've *gotta have some of your attention.*
   a. "Promises, Promises"/Naked Eyes
   b. "Brass in Pocket"/Pretenders

    c. "Call Me"/Blondie

7. They wonder what you are going to do *when every-body's insane.*

    a. "Crazy on You"/Heart
    b. "Emotional Rescue"/Rolling Stones
    c. "(She's) Sexy + 17"/Stray Cats

8. Something deep inside tells them to go ahead and call her—to *just close* their *eyes and she'll be there.*

    a. "Something"/Beatles
    b. "Pretty Ballerina"/Left Banke
    c. "Younger Girl"/Critters

9. They *turn on some music to start* their *day,* lose themselves *in a familiar song,* then close their *eyes and slip away.*

    a. "Juke Box Hero"/Foreigner
    b. "Rock 'n' Roll Fantasy"/Bad Company
    c. "More Than a Feeling"/Boston

10. They wonder whether time will *make man more wise.*

    a. "Time"/Sunshine Company
    b. "Time Has Come Today"/Chambers Brothers
    c. "Shapes of Things"/Yardbirds

11. They want you to do this *to the music* so they can have *time to breathe.*

    a. "Dance to the Music"/Sly and the Family Stone
    b. "Stop! Stop! Stop!"/Hollies
    c. "Listen to the Music"/Doobie Brothers

12. He *never knew a better time,* and he probably *never will.*

    a. "Vincent"/Don McLean
    b. "Walk on the Wild Side"/Lou Reed
    c. "Crocodile Rock"/Elton John

13. *Romeo and Juliet are together in eternity.*

    a. "Bungle in the Jungle"/Jethro Tull

    b. "(Don't Fear) the Reaper"/Blue Öyster Cult

    c. "We've Got Tonite"/Bob Seger and the Silver Bullet Band

14. They say that, *like the flame that burns the candle, the candle feeds the flame.*

    a. "Keep the Fire Burnin'"/REO Speedwagon

    b. "You Make My Dreams"/Daryl Hall and John Oates

    c. "Don't Stop Believin'"/Journey

15. They advise you to *take time to make time* and *make time to be there.*

    a. "Lady"/Little River Band

    b. "Games People Play"/Alan Parsons Project

    c. "Let 'Em In"/Wings

16. The *day destroys the night, the night divides the day.*

    a. "Break On Through to the Other Side"/Doors

    b. "There's a Kind of Hush"/Herman's Hermits

    c. "Here Comes the Night"/Them

17. *When you put on your makeup,* be sure others see *your good side.*

    a. "Goody Two Shoes"/Adam Ant

    b. "Cruel to Be Kind"/Nick Lowe

    c. "Mama Can't Buy You Love"/Elton John

18. *Textile mills are closing down,* not the way it used to be.

    a. "Pink Houses"/John Cougar Mellencamp

    b. "My Hometown"/Bruce Springsteen

    c. "Perfect World"/Huey Lewis and the News

19. They notice the *lions and tigers who wait in the shadows* and who *sleep in green meadows.*

    a. "Bungle in the Jungle"/Jethro Tull

    b. "Junior's Farm"/Wings

    c. "Joy to the World"/Three Dog Night

20. Can't you see that they're *desperate* because they *get high just being around you.*

    a. "I Need You"/Beatles
    b. "I Think I Love You"/Partridge Family
    c. "Sit Down, I Think I Love You"/Mojo Men

21. She *knows how to rock and roll* and gives them *hot and cold fever.*
    a. "Jump"/Van Halen
    b. "Christine Sixteen"/Kiss
    c. "Crazy Little Thing Called Love"/Queen

22. They *don't have to love* him as long as they can *get high awhile.*
    a. "Rapture"/Blondie
    b. "Show Me"/Pretenders
    c. "Magic Man"/Heart

23. *When you look through the years,* they say *your wife seems to think you're part of the furniture.*
    a. "Reeling in the Years"/Steely Dan
    b. "Reminiscing"/Little River Band
    c. "Take the Long Way Home"/Supertramp

24. They ask if you can hear other people talking about them, adding that *it doesn't matter anyway* because it's only *jealous games people play.*
    a. "Don't Stand So Close to Me"/Police
    b. "Our Lips Are Sealed"/Go-Go's
    c. "Any Way You Want It"/Journey

25. They say *it's a crime* and say you should *share it* as long as you *don't take a slice of* their *pie.*
    a. "Easy Livin"/Uriah Heep
    b. "Miracles"/Jefferson Starship
    c. "Money"/Pink Floyd

26. They're *not asking for much* and simply want someone to take them *downtown.*
    a. "Tush"/ZZ Top
    b. "Waiting on a Friend"/Rolling Stones

    c. "Band on the Run"/Paul McCartney and Wings

27. They want him to *play a tune* to *make* them *happy.*
    a. "Happy Jack"/Who
    b. "Dear Mr. Fantasy"/Traffic
    c. "Mr. Tambourine Man"/Byrds

28. They start *singing to the beat* when they see you *walking down the street.*
    a. "Sha La La"/Manfred Mann
    b. "Can't You Hear My Heart Beat"/Herman's Hermits
    c. "Let's Live for Today"/Grass Roots

29. They wonder *what kind of girl is this who's never ever been kissed?*
    a. "What Kind of Girl Is This"/Joey Dee and the Starlighters
    b. "Respectable"/Outsiders
    c. "Are You a Boy or Are You a Girl?"/Barbarians

30. His *stallion stands in need of company.*
    a. "Conquistador"/Procol Harum
    b. "A Horse With No Name"/America
    c. "Back in the Saddle"/Aerosmith

31. They advise you not to *say words you're gonna regret* or *let the fire rush to your head.*
    a. "Harden My Heart"/Quarterflash
    b. "Eye in the Sky"/Alan Parsons Project
    c. "Take It Easy on Me"/Little River Band

32. If you leave, they tell you not to telephone because, since they *need someone to make* them *feel better,* they *won't be alone.*
    a. "Blue Morning, Blue Day"/Foreigner
    b. "Lovin', Touchin', Squeezin'"/Journey
    c. "Don't Look Back"/Boston

33. *It's just a matter of time before you make up your mind* and give them all *the love that you've been hiding.*

    a. "Sooner or Later"/Grass Roots
    b. "No Sugar Tonight"/Guess Who
    c. "Let Me"/Paul Revere and the Raiders

34. They warn you that *you'd better watch your step, or start living with your mother.*

    a. "Hey Joe"/Leaves
    b. "Run for Your Life"/Beatles
    c. "Play With Fire"/Rolling Stones

35. *Breathe deep.*

    a. "Nights in White Satin"/Moody Blues
    b. "Piece of My Heart"/Big Brother and the Holding Company
    c. "The Air That I Breathe"/Hollies

36. There are *1352 guitar pickers.*

    a. "Monterey"/Animals
    b. "Nashville Cats"/Lovin' Spoonful
    c. "Rock and Roll Heaven"/Righteous Brothers

37. When *she looked at him with those soft eyes, so innocent and blue,* the boy *knew right then he was too far from home.*

    a. "New Kid in Town"/Eagles
    b. "Hollywood Nights"/Bob Seger and the Silver Bullet Band
    c. "What a Fool Believes"/Doobie Brothers

38. It *always wins.*

    a. "Heart and Soul"/Huey Lewis and the News
    b. "Authority Song"/John Cougar Mellencamp
    c. "Body Language"/Queen

39. They say that *you can blame it all on* them because they *just can't live without you.*

    a. "I Want to Know What Love Is"/Foreigner
    b. "Say It Isn't So"/Daryl Hall and John Oates
    c. "Baby Come Back"/Player

40. Their advice is to *look at yourself.*
    a. "I Can See for Miles"/Who
    b. "You Better Move On"/Rolling Stones
    c. "Incense and Peppermints"/Strawberry Alarm Clock

41. They say that it's *very nice to know* that she *ain't got no place left to go.*
    a. "If You Leave Me Now"/Chicago
    b. "Crazy Love"/Poco
    c. "Evil Woman"/Electric Light Orchestra

42. They were *so much older then,* but they're *younger than that now.*
    a. "My Back Pages"/Byrds
    b. "When I Was Young"/Animals
    c. "Happenings Ten Years Time Ago"/Yardbirds

43. He *gets up in the evening* with *nothin' to say,* then comes home *in the morning* and goes to bed *feeling the same way.*
    a. "Dancing in the Dark"/Bruce Springsteen
    b. "Affair of the Heart"/Rick Springfield
    c. "Heart to Heart"/Kenny Loggins

44. They want to know if you'll *come upstairs* and *have a drink of champagne.*
    a. "Flirtin' With Disaster"/Molly Hatchet
    b. "What's Your Name"/Lynyrd Skynyrd
    c. "Sleeping Bag"/ZZ Top

45. He's *going back to a place that's far away* but he wonders if you've *got a place to stay.*
    a. "Show Me the Way"/Jackson Browne
    b. "We Just Disagree"/Dave Mason

    c. "Margaritaville"/Jimmy Buffett

46. She *holds her head so high, like a statue in the sky.*
    a. "Arizona"/Mark Lindsay
    b. "Foxy Lady"/Jimi Hendrix
    c. "Hello, I Love You"/Doors

47. *She was walkin' down the street, lookin' fine as she could be.*
    a. "She's About a Mover"/Sir Douglas Quintet
    b. "Do Wah Diddy Diddy"/Manfred Mann
    c. "Sweet Little Sixteen"/Chuck Berry

48. Because she's *growing up so fast*, their mama's *worrying that she won't last.*
    a. "Suzanne"/Journey
    b. "Mothers Talk"/Tears for Fears
    c. "Sister Christian"/Night Ranger

49. They say that, *in conversations, she spoke just like a Baroness.*
    a. "Lady"/Styx
    b. "Jackie Blue"/Ozark Mountain Daredevils
    c. "Killer Queen"/Queen

50. They want you to *sing for the laughter* and *sing for the tears.*
    a. "Bad Time"/Grand Funk
    b. "Immigrant Song"/Led Zeppelin
    c. "Dream On"/Aerosmith

51. They *shed a million tears for you,* and *now you're loving someone new.*
    a. "Lies"/Knickerbockers
    b. "You've Lost That Lovin' Feeling"/Righteous Brothers
    c. "96 Tears"/? and the Mysterians

52. They want to *take you down to the riverbed* and tell you something that will *go right to your head.*

    a. "Sunshine of Your Love"/Cream
    b. "I Got a Line on You"/Spirit
    c. "Magic Carpet Ride"/Steppenwolf

53. Once *every boy and girl* was their friend, but in today's revolution people *don't know what they're fighting.*
    a. "I'd Love to Change the World"/Ten Years After
    b. "Living in the Past"/Jethro Tull
    c. "Whatever Gets You Thru the Night"/John Lennon and the Plastic Ono Band

54. *The spinning room is sinking deep* as they're *waiting for the break of day.*
    a. "25 or 6 to 4"/Chicago
    b. "A Whiter Shade of Pale"/Procol Harum
    c. "Hocus Pocus"/Focus

55. They say *it took so long just to realize* they're *much too strong to compromise.*
    a. "Biggest Part of Me"/Ambrosia
    b. "Don't Look Back"/Boston
    c. "Come Dancing"/Kinks

56. He says you've *got to do what you can just to keep your love alive.*
    a. "Fly Like an Eagle"/Steve Miller
    b. "Running on Empty"/Jackson Browne
    c. "Time Passages"/Al Stewart

57. She tells him to *just shut* his *mouth.*
    a. "China Girl"/David Bowie
    b. "Uptown Girl"/Billy Joel
    c. "Little Jeannie"/Elton John

58. They get their lovin' one night a week, and *it's a good thing they don't bottle the stuff!*
    a. "Good Lovin'"/Young Rascals
    b. "Love Potion Number Nine"/Searchers

    c. "Double Shot"/Swingin' Medallions

59. They'll be *playing with the boys all night.*

    a. "We're an American Band"/Grand Funk Railroad

    b. "Beth"/Kiss

    c. "We Are the Champions"/Queen

60. *Tonight she'll be so exciting* because they *want her all for* themselves.

    a. "Temptation Eyes"/Grass Roots

    b. "All My Lovin'"/Beatles

    c. "Let's Spend the Night Together"/Rolling Stones

61. If you *make a wish,* they say that *love will make it come true.*

    a. "Here I Am"/Air Supply

    b. "You Can Do Magic"/America

    c. "Biggest Part of Me"/Ambrosia

62. They want to *get back* to their *city by the bay.*

    a. "Lights"/Journey

    b. "I Can't Hold Back"/Survivor

    c. "Faithfully"/Foreigner

63. He spends *so much time believing all the lies to keep the dream alive.*

    a. "One More Night"/Phil Collins

    b. "I Can Dream About You"/Dan Hartman

    c. "Eyes Without a Face"/Billy Idol

64. *Your nose is longer than a telephone wire.*

    a. "Liar, Liar"/Castaways

    b. "Psychotic Reaction"/Count Five

    c. "Everybody Knows"/Dave Clark Five

65. Although you *hurt* them *to* their *soul,* they still feel with *every breath* and *every move* that they *can't let you go.*

    a. "Every Breath You Take"/Police

    b. "D'yer Maker"/Led Zeppelin

    c. "Free Ride"/Edgar Winter Group

66. If you told him *you were drowning,* he *would not lend a hand.*
    a. "Dirty Laundry"/Don Henley
    b. "Fade Away"/Bruce Springsteen
    c. "In the Air Tonight"/Phil Collins

67. According to them, it's *you and me who killed the Kennedys.*
    a. "2 + 2 = ?"/Bob Seger System
    b. "Revolution"/Beatles
    c. "Sympathy for the Devil"/Rolling Stones

68. If you *build your house,* they ask you to *please call* them.
    a. "Sara"/Fleetwood Mac
    b. "Don't Stop Believing"/Journey
    c. "High on You"/Survivor

69. *Reflections in the waves spark memories: some happy, some sad.*
    a. "Long Long Way From Home"/Foreigner
    b. "Come Sail Away"/Styx
    c. "I Won't Hold You Back"/Toto

70. They want to *sail away,* and ask you to give them *two good reasons why* they *ought to stay.*
    a. "Sunny Afternoon"/Kinks
    b. "Time Won't Let Me"/Outsiders
    c. "Last Train to Clarksville"/Monkees

71. They wonder where they go from here *now that all of the children have grown.*
    a. "Isn't It Time"/Babys
    b. "Reminiscing"/Little River Band
    c. "Games People Play"/Alan Parsons Project

72. They'll wait *where the shadows run from themselves.*
    a. "Pictures of Matchstick Men"/Status Quo

    b. "White Room"/Cream

    c. "7 and 7 Is"/Love

73. They were *cut loose like a deuce.*

    a. "Blinded by the Light"/Manfred Mann's Earth Band

    b. "Miracles"/Jefferson Starship

    c. "Rock This Town"/Stray Cats

74. Because *your sorrow is all* they see, they feel that *if you just want to cry to somebody, don't cry to* them.

    a. "Take the Long Way Home"/Supertramp

    b. "Run Run Run"/Jo Jo Gunne

    c. "Strange Way"/Firefall

75. Sometimes he feels *like the whole human race.*

    a. "When Doves Cry"/Prince

    b. "Blue Jean"/David Bowie

    c. "Against All Odds (Take a Look at Me Now)"/Phil Collins

76. They say that *your armor has long since lost its sheen.*

    a. "Albert Flasher"/Guess Who

    b. "Conquistador"/Procol Harum

    c. "Mr. Bojangles"/Nitty Gritty Dirt Band

77. He could see that *she was keeping a secret fire* and if he *got real close,* he'd burn.

    a. "How Much Love"/Leo Sayer

    b. "Ebony Eyes"/Bob Welch

    c. "Hot Child in the City"/Nick Gilder

78. They wonder why you *won't talk about the reasons why you and* they *fight.*

    a. "Don't Let It End"/Styx

    b. "Head Games"/Foreigner

    c. "Set Me Free"/Utopia

79. They want to *bring dynamite and a crane* to blow the place up and start again.

   a. "We Gotta Get Out of This Place"/Animals
   b. "Tobacco Road"/Nashville Teens
   c. "Love Street"/Doors

80. *Though we rush ahead to save our time, we are only what we feel.*
   a. "On the Way Home"/Buffalo Springfield
   b. "My Back Pages"/Byrds
   c. "Yellow Balloon"/Yellow Balloon

81. There are times when *questions run too deep for such a simple man.*
   a. "Maybe I'm Amazed"/Wings
   b. "The Logical Song"/Supertramp
   c. "Just Remember I Love You"/Firefall

82. They wonder *how many years* it will take *for people to be free.*
   a. "People Got to Be Free"/Rascals
   b. "Blowin' in the Wind"/Peter, Paul and Mary
   c. "The World Is a Ghetto"/War

83. If you *give back your ring* to them, they'll *set you free* to *go with him.*
   a. "Set Me Free"/Kinks
   b. "Go Now"/Moody Blues
   c. "Anna"/Beatles

84. Because *the revolution's near,* they warn us that *we have got to get it together now.*
   a. "I Can See for Miles"/Who
   b. "Something in the Air"/Thunderclap Newman
   c. "Get Together"/Youngbloods

85. *Nobody could save him* when a *bullet had found him,* so *he lay down and he died.*
   a. "Lucky Man"/Emerson, Lake and Palmer
   b. "Lonely Boy"/Andrew Gold
   c. "Indiana Wants Me"/R. Dean Taylor

86. Because time isn't on their side, they want to *burn out the day* and *burn out the night.*
   a. "Burning Down the House"/Talking Heads
   b. "Burnin' for You"/Blue Öyster Cult
   c. "Burning Heart"/Survivor

87. *You can't be twenty* here even *though you're thinking that you're leaving there too soon.*
   a. "Alice's Restaurant"/Arlo Guthrie
   b. "Sugar Mountain"/Neil Young
   c. "Desolation Row"/Bob Dylan

88. All they want is to *just be free* and *live their life the way* they *want to be.*
   a. "Not the Lovin' Kind"/Dino, Desi and Billy
   b. "I Wanna Be Free"/Monkees
   c. "Pushin' Too Hard"/Seeds

89. *Out in the streets* and *out in the playground is the dark side of town.*
   a. "Africa"/Toto
   b. "Don't Talk to Strangers"/Rick Springfield
   c. "Electric Avenue"/Eddy Grant

90. Someone waiting at your door will tell you that *darkness gives you much more than you get from the light.*
   a. "1984"/Spirit
   b. "Hey Big Brother"/Rare Earth
   c. "Murder in My Heart for the Judge"/Moby Grape

91. Although you say you're his friend, he's at his *wit's end* because your love doesn't *coincide with the things you do.*
   a. "Straight From the Heart"/Bryan Adams
   b. "Cruel to Be Kind"/Nick Lowe
   c. "Little Jeannie"/Elton John

92. Tonight, *in the darkness*, they want to *give it all to you* and *lay it at your feet.*

    a. "I Was Made for Lovin' You"/Kiss

    b. "Jane"/Jefferson Starship

    c. "I Want You to Want Me"/Cheap Trick

93. They *hear the talking of the deejay* though they really don't know what he's saying.

    a. "Mexican Radio"/Wall of Voodoo

    b. "Kokomo"/Beach Boys

    c. "I Love Rock 'N Roll"/Joan Jett and the Blackhearts

94. They've got a dirty mind because they *always get it up for the younger kind.*

    a. "My Sharona"/Knack

    b. "Senses Working Overtime"/XTC

    c. "One Thing Leads to Another"/Fixx

95. They want you to *roll them in designer sheets* because they *never get enough.*

    a. "Call Me"/Blondie

    b. "Hot Summer Nights"/Night

    c. "Vacation"/Go-Go's

96. In their dream, they *touched your golden hair and tasted your perfume.*

    a. "(We Ain't Got) Nothin' Yet"/Blues Magoos

    b. "I Had Too Much to Dream"/Electric Prunes

    c. "Pretty Ballerina"/Left Banke

97. You ran out on them, *so other girls did it, too.*

    a. "Morning Girl"/Neon Philharmonic

    b. "Little Girl"/Syndicate of Sound

    c. "Steppin' Out"/Paul Revere and the Raiders

98. From this trip there's a chance, they warn, that *you might not come back.*

    a. "In-A Gadda-Da-Vida"/Iron Butterfly

    b. "Journey to the Center of the Mind"/Amboy Dukes

    c. "Dead Man's Curve"/Jan and Dean

99. Because they're *up to here in lies,* their *name is really mud.*
    a.   "Lies"/Knickerbockers
    b.   "Silence Is Golden"/Tremeloes
    c.   "Talk, Talk"/Music Machine

100. *Seven horses are on the march.*
    a.   "All Along the Watchtower"/Jimi Hendrix
    b.   "The Rains Came"/Sir Douglas Quintet
    c.   "Love Her Madly"/Doors

V

Rock of Ages:
Tomorrow's Classic Rockers

The following questions are from rock hits of the mid-eighties and early nineties that I feel are destined to herald the next era of Classic Rock and Roll!

In 1958 Danny and the Juniors crowed, "rock and roll is here to stay," and forty years later there's no denying that it's as strong as ever before. It'll continue to survive and thrive even through times of uncertainty and change. As the eternal Meat Loaf himself said, "When we really need it most, that's when rock-and-roll dreams come through." Long live rock and roll!

Lyrics

1. What do the Romantics hear while you're "Talking in Your Sleep"?
   a. the secrets that you keep
   b. gurgling sounds from the deep
   c. something about love and sheep

2. In "Karma Chameleon," what are the colors of the dreams of Culture Club?
   a. bright orange and yellow
   b. red, gold, and green
   c. black and blue

3. In "I'm Gonna Be (500 Miles)," what do the Proclaimers say they'd do after walking five hundred miles?
   a. walk five hundred more
   b. knock on your door
   c. be sure they stay that far away from you

4. What did "The Sign" do for Ace of Base?
   a. it sent them running for shelter
   b. it opened up their eyes
   c. it made them love you even more

5. In "Hungry Eyes," what does Eric Carmen feel between you and him?
   a. the heat
   b. a wall of indifference
   c. the magic

6. What word describes how you sounded to the Jets in "Rocket 2 U" when you told them to come over?
   a. infatuated
   b. frantic
   c. drunk

7. In "Simply Irresistible," what word does Robert Palmer use to describe that kind of love?
   a. mythical
   b. magnetic
   c. wonderful

8. What happens to Sheriff "When I'm With You"?
   a. the act foolish and silly
   b. they get chills
   c. they feel funny inside

9. In "I Can't Hold Back," what can Survivor feel you do when they touch you?
   a. relax and open up
   b. hold them tightly
   c. tremble

10. When Kenny Loggins becomes "Footloose," what does he want to kick off?
    a. the blues
    b. his Sunday shoes
    c. his two left feet

11. In "Kyrie," what did Mr. Mister use to think about when they were young?
    a. running away
    b. being rich

   c. growing old

12. Where does ABC tell you to shoot that "Poison Arrow"?
   a. through their heart
   b. into the air
   c. at the moon

13. In "Low," what does Cracker say being with you is like?
   a. riding in a jet airplane
   b. drowning in the middle of the sea
   c. being stoned

14. In "Found Out About You," what do the Gin Blossoms say follows you everywhere you go?
   a. love
   b. muddy tracks
   c. rumors

15. How do Guns 'N Roses describe "Paradise City"?
   a. as a place where all the cats are looking for a kitty
   b. it's where the grass is green and the girls are pretty
   c. it's a town without pity

16. Because they are the "Man in the Box," what does Alice in Chains want you to do for them?
   a. save them
   b. give them away to someone who really cares
   c. untie the ropes and let them breathe

17. According to Pearl Jam, what didn't daddy do for "Jeremy"?
   a. pick him up from school on time
   b. give him attention or affection
   c. treat him right

18. In "Smells Like Teen Spirit," how is Nirvana acting?
   a. cautious and suspicious

    b.   carefree and delicious

    c.   stupid and contagious

19. Because he's a "Loser," what does Beck want you to do?

    a.   help him learn to win

    b.   be his guiding light

    c.   kill him

20. If you "Dance Naked," what does John Mellencamp promise not to do?

    a.   touch you

    b.   laugh at you

    c.   join you

21. Because they're at the "Point of No Return," what does Exposé want to do?

    a.   call you on the phone

    b.   take you in their arms

    c.   go all the way

22. In "Shattered Dreams," how did Johnny Hates Jazz find the future to be looking when they woke up?

    a.   shiny as a rainbow

    b.   in bits and pieces

    c.   not so bright

23. In "New Sensation," what does INXS say is written all over your face?

    a.   excuses

    b.   dirty thoughts

    c.   love

24. Because they feel "Everybody Wants to Rule the World," what do Tears for Fears accuse you of doing?

    a.   turning your back on Mother Nature

    b.   trying to lead other people's lives

    c.   selling out to society

25. According to Bon Jovi, who are the couple who are "Livin' on a Prayer?"

   a. Jill and Johnny
   b. Gerry and Jermaine
   c. Tommy and Gina

26. Because they're so "Crazy" about you, what does your kind of lovin' make Aerosmith want to do?
   a. pull down the shades
   b. scream and shout to everyone
   c. hang themselves from the tree of love

27. In "Rock and Roll Girls," what does John Fogerty sometimes think life is?
   a. a fantasy land
   b. a hot vacation
   c. a rodeo

28. What does Scritti Politti have the "Perfect Way" to do?
   a. say goodbye
   b. make the girls go crazy
   c. make money

29. How old was Jane's Addiction when they first "Been Caught Stealing"?
   a. five
   b. ten
   c. thirteen

30. In "Right Now," what does Van Halen say happens if you miss the beat?
   a. you fall behind
   b. you lose the rhythm
   c. you dance to another song

31. What do Men Without Hats say we can do with our friends when we dance "The Safety Dance,"
   a. be safe
   b. anything we want to do
   c. leave them behind.

32. In "Something's Always Wrong," where is it that Toad the Wet Sprocket say you and they always seem to meet?

   a. at the wrong floor
   b. where love has no place
   c. in the spaces in between

33. What does Night Ranger tell "Sister Christian"?

   a. that she's growing up too fast
   b. that she's a sinner
   c. that there's more to life than meets the eye

34. In "All That She Wants," what does Ace of Base say it's a day for doing?

   a. talking over the telephone
   b. lying on the beach and having fun
   c. nothing

35. In "Cut Your Hair," what does Pavement say they see starting up each and every day?

   a. new bands
   b. wars and civil strife
   c. passionate fires

36. According to Green Day in "Longview," what don't they have?

   a. a friend
   b. motivation
   c. hassles and hangups

37. In "Vasoline," what do Stone Temple Pilots ay they'd be if they were all alone?

   a. lonely
   b. safer
   c. forgotten

38. In "Shine," what does Collective Soul ask you to show them?

   a. where the batteries can be found

    b. where to look

    c. a way out

39. Because they're "Human," what does Human League say they were born to do?

    a. suffer

    b. love you

    c. make mistakes

40. In "Head Like a Hole," what do Nine Inch Nails want you to do?

    a. search the street and alleys for the girl you think you need

    b. pick yourself up and see the light

    c. bow down before the one you serve

41. In "Man on the Moon," what does R.E.M. want to play?

    a. Twister and Risk

    b. all their old hit singles

    c. cowboys and Indians

42. According to Counting Crows in "Mr. Jones," what is their favorite color?

    a. grey

    b. marsh green

    c. lavender

43. In "Mysterious Ways," what does U2 say you'd better do if you want to kiss the sky?

    a. talk the talk

    b. fly

    c. learn how to kneel

44. According to Candlebox, what is for "You"?

    a. all their love

    b. the blood on their hands

    c. all the mysteries of life unseen

45. In "Sad But True," what does Metallica say they'll be when you want love?

    a. your hand
    b. your hate
    c. your dream

46. What does Bruce Springsteen say has vanished on the "Streets of Philadelphia"?
    a. voices of friends
    b. sickness and poverty
    c. the sounds of the city

47. In "I've Been Thinking About You," how does Londonbeat still feel deep down inside?
    a. warm and fuzzy
    b. funny
    c. confused

48. In "Until I Fall Away," what is the Gin Blossoms' fear?
    a. that they'll be stuck in this town forever
    b. that they'll never be in love again
    c. that others won't understand their words

49. Because they're a "Liar," what will Rollins Band hide behind?
    a. a smile
    b. your deepest fears
    c. a mirror

50. In "The Future's So Bright, I Gotta Wear Shades," what is Timbuk 3 studying in school?
    a. nuclear science
    b. Success 101
    c. Leisure 201

Titles

1. They *called you up in the middle of the night* because they were a *key that could use a little turning.*
    a. "Into Your Arms"/Lemonheads

   b. "I Don't Want to Live Without You"/Foreigner
   c. "Runaway Train"/Soul Asylum

2. *The lightbulb's getting dim* and *there's meltdown in the sky.*
   a. "November Rain"/Guns 'N Roses
   b. "Livin' on the Edge"/Aerosmith
   c. "Give It Away"/Red Hot Chili Peppers

3. They wonder *how we can dance while our world keeps turning.*
   a. "Stand"/R.E.M.
   b. "When the Children Cry"/White Lion
   c. "Beds Are Burning"/Midnight Oil

4. Because they're *half the man* they *used to be,* they ask you to *take time with a wounded hand.*
   a. "Creep"/Stone Temple Pilots
   b. "Alive"/Pearl Jam
   c. "Come As You Are"/Nirvana

5. Every time he *closes his eyes,* he *sees your face.*
   a. "I'd Do Anything for Love (But I Won't Do That)"/Meat Loaf
   b. "If Ever I Lose My Faith in You"/Sting
   c. "Tears in Heaven"/Eric Clapton

6. They ask you to *shove* them *in the shallow water before* they *get too deep.*
   a. "Say You Will"/Foreigner
   b. "Point of No Return"/Exposé
   c. "What I Am"/Edie Brickell and the New Bohemians

7. Though they've *said too much,* they feel they *haven't said enough.*
   a. "Comedown"/Bush
   b. "Losing My Religion"/R.E.M.
   c. "Higher Ground"/UB40

8. They *feel it in* their *fingers* and *in* their *toes.*

    a. "Love Is All Around"/Wet Wet Wet

    b. "Only Wanna Be With You"/Hootie and the Blowfish

    c. "Friday I'm in Love"/Cure

  9. It's hard for them *to believe that* they're *all alone*.

    a. "Have You Ever Needed Someone So Bad"/Def Leppard

    b. "Disappear"/INXS

    c. "Under the Bridge"/Red Hot Chili Peppers

10. Words *are very unnecessary*.

    a. "Enjoy the Silence"/Depeche Mode

    b. "Love Song"/Tesla

    c. "Price of Love"/Bad English

11. All they can say is their *life is pretty plain*.

    a. "Dumb"/Nirvana

    b. "No Rain"/Blind Melon

    c. "Runaway Train"/Soul Asylum

12. Love *can make you blind* and *make you act so strange*.

    a. "Everyday"/Phil Collins

    b. "Come Undone"/Duran Duran.

    c. "Stay" (I Missed You)"/Lisa Loeb and Nine Stories

13. *Now the music's on*, they wonder why you don't dance with them.

    a. "Don't You Want Me"/Human League

    b. "Everybody Have Fun Tonight"/Wang Chung

    c. "What Have I Done to Deserve This?"/Pet Shop Boys

14. *Out on the road today*, he *saw a Deadhead sticker on a Cadillac*.

    a. "Born in the U.S.A."/Bruce Springsteen

    b. "Little Red Corvette"/Prince

    c. "The Boys of Summer"/Don Henley

15. *Once upon a time*, they *remember skies reflecting in your eyes*.

    a. "King for a Day"/Thompson Twins

    b. "Your Wildest Dreams"/Moody Blues

    c. "These Dreams"/Heart

16. They've got *one more time to kill the pain.*

    a. "J.A.R."/Green Day

    b. "Mary Jane's Last Dance"/Tom Petty and the Heartbreakers

    c. "'Til I Hear It From You"/Gin Blossoms

17. After they *tuck you in,* you sleep *with one eye open.*

    a. "Enter Sandman"/Metallica

    b. "Because the Night"/10,000 Maniacs

    c. "Paradise City"/Guns 'N Roses

18. He wants you to take him *over the edge.*

    a. "Make Me Lose Control"/Eric Carmen

    b. "Danger Zone"/Kenny Loggins

    c. "R.O.C.K. in the U.S.A."/John Cougar Mellencamp

19. They *tried so hard not to get upset* because they *know all the trouble* they'll *get.*

    a. "Careless Whisper"/Wham!

    b. "You Might Think"/Cars

    c. "Voices Carry"/'Til Tuesday

20. They *swear* they *don't have a gun.*

    a. "Tennessee"/Arrested Development

    b. "Found Out About You"/Gin Blossoms

    c. "Come As You Are"/Nirvana

21. Some *sweat when the heat is on.*

    a. "Danger Zone"/Kenny Loggins

    b. "Some Like It Hot"/Power Station

    c. "The Heat Is On"/Glen Frey

22. Once there was a girl who wouldn't change with the other girls, and when they made her, *they saw birthmarks all over her body.*

    a. "All That She Wants"/Ace of Base

    b. "Three Little Pigs"/Green Jelly

    c. "Mmm Mmm Mmm Mmm"/Crash Test Dummies

23. They wonder if you can remember when they *lost the keys and you lost more than that* to them.

    a. "Never Say Goodbye"/Bon Jovi

    b. "Sweet Child O' Mine"/Guns 'N Roses

    c. "Drive"/Cars

24. *She'll tell you she's an orphan after you meet her family.*

    a. "She Talks to Angels"/Black Crowes

    b. "Rebirth of Slick (Cool Like Dat)"/Digable Planets

    c. "Round Here"/Counting Crows

25. They *love her eyes and her wild wild hair.*

    a. "Wild Wild Life"/Talking Heads

    b. "The Wild Boys"/Duran Duran

    c. "Wild, Wild West"/Escape Club

26. If you *don't expect too much* from them, *you might not be let down.*

    a. "I'm Gonna Be (500 Miles)"/Proclaimers

    b. "Hey Jealousy"/Gin Blossoms

    c. "Shiny Happy People"/R.E.M.

27. *You don't have to watch Dynasty to have an attitude.*

    a. "Kiss"/Prince

    b. "Hangin' Tough"/New Kids on the Block

    c. "All About Soul"/Billy Joel

28. All their *friends are brown and red.*

    a. "Bad Boys"/Inner Circle

    b. "Spoonman"/Soundgarden

    c. "Two Princes"/Spin Doctors

29. They *won't harm you or touch your defenses, vanity, or insecurity.*

    a. "Safety Dance"/Men Without Hats

    b. "Freedom"/Wham!

   c. "Don't You (Forget About Me)"/Simple Minds

30. *You want it all, but you can't have it.*
   a. "Real, Real, Real"/Jesus Jones
   b. "Epic"/Faith No More
   c. "Wind of Change"/Scorpions

31. They *need you now* before they *lose* their *mind.*
   a. "Need You Tonight"/INXS
   b. "More Than Words Can Say"/Alias
   c. "Hold On"/Wilson Phillips

32. He's *playing this game* and he *won't stop until* he's *done.*
   a. "Wicked Game"/Chris Isaak
   b. "Hazard"/Richard Marx
   c. "Are You Gonna Go My Way"/Lenny Kravitz

33. You *make them hungry* again because *everything you do is irresistible.*
   a. "Born to Be My Baby"/Bon Jovi
   b. "Why Can't I Be You"/Cure
   c. "You Got It (The Right Stuff)"/New Kids on the Block

34. They wonder *how high* you can *fly with broken wings.*
   a. "Amazing"/Aerosmith
   b. "High Enough"/Damn Yankees
   c. "Losing My Religion"/.R.E.M.

35. You and they *make a beautiful team.*
   a. "Shine"/Collective Soul
   b. "7"/Prince and the New Generation
   c. "Love Is Strong"/Rolling Stones

36. He wonders *what are you concealing* and asks you to *give* him *a sign.*
   a. "Say Something"/James
   b. "Please Forgive Me"/Bryan Adams
   c. "The River of Dreams"/Billy Joel

37. There's *something about you that makes* them *sweat.*
    a. "Need You Tonight"/INXS
    b. "Nothin' But a Good Time"/Poison
    c. "I Feel You"/Depeche Mode

38. They say that *we live our lives by all those things we say and do.*
    a. "Never a Time"/Phil Collins and Genesis
    b. "All for Love"/Bryan Adams, Rod Stewart, and Sting
    c. "Don't Turn Around"/Ace of Base

39. *The killer in them is the killer in you.*
    a. "Sad But True"/Metallica
    b. "Mysterious Ways"/U2
    c. "Disarm"/Smashing Pumpkins

40. They say that *you ought to know that girl by now* because she's the kind that will *never settle down.*
    a. "You Let Your Heart Go Too Fast"/Spin Doctors
    b. "Linger"/Cranberries
    c. "Two Steps Behind"/Def Leppard

41. He come from *a small town* where the people *think so small* and use small words.
    a. "Another Day in Paradise"/Phil Collins
    b. "Roll With It"/Steve Winwood
    c. "Big Time"/Peter Gabriel

42. She *loves Jesus and America, too* and is *crazy about Elvis.*
    a. "Pop Singer"/John Cougar Mellencamp
    b. "Free Fallin'"/Tom Petty
    c. "My Hometown"/Bruce Springsteen

43. They say that *someday he'll begin his life again.*
    a. "Evenflow"/Pearl Jam
    b. "Livin' on the Edge"/Aerosmith
    c. "Mr. Wendal"/Arrested Development

44. They wonder why people *don't do what they say* or *say what they mean.*
   a. "People Are People"/Depeche Mode
   b. "One Thing Leads to Anothe /Fixx
   c. "Separate Ways"/Journey

45. You *can't run away forever, but there's nothing wrong with getting a good head start.*
   a. "Are You Gonna Go My Way"/Lenny Kravitz
   b. "Rock and Roll Dreams Come Through"/Meat Loaf
   c. "Wild Night"/John Mellencamp with Me'Shell Ndegeocello

46. Here they've got *fun and games* and *everything you want.*
   a. "Perfect World"/Huey Lewis and the News
   b. "Welcome to the Jungle"/Guns 'N Roses
   c. "Tom's Diner"/D.N.A. featuring Suzanne Vega

47. Making love to you *might drive* them *crazy.*
   a. "Doctor! Doctor!"/Mike + the Mechanics
   c. "Love Bites"/Def Leppard

48. They are *cast from Eden's gate with no regrets.*
   a. "I'd Die for You"/Bon Jovi
   b. "The Unforgiven"/Metallica
   c. "Every Rose Has Its Thorn"/Poison

49. Although they might be *destroyed by MTV,* they wouldn't want to *bite the hand that feeds.*
   a. "Too Much Information"/Duran Duran
   b. "Money for Nothing"/Dire Straits
   c. "Hold Me Now"/Thompson Twins

50. His boss, *Mr. McGee,* didn't like him because he worked *a bit too leisurely.*
   a. "Jack and Diane"/John Cougar
   b. "Born in the U.S.A."/Bruce Springsteen
   c. "Raspberry Beret"/Prince

Answers

From Aerosmith to ZZ Top:
Classic Rock Artist Questions

Aerosmith

1. **b.** "Sweet Emotion" (in 1975)
2. **b.** *Sgt. Pepper's Lonely Hearts Club Band*
3. **a.** "Walk This Way" (repopularized with the aid of Run-D.M.C.)
4. **b.** where they'll be in a year
5. **a.** in books

Air Supply

1. **b.** Australia
2. **a.** "The One That You Love"
3. **c.** that they were the lonely ones
4. **a.** ride the skies
5. **b.** memories

America

1. **b.** Neil Young, whose "Heart of Gold" had also just climbed to number one on the music charts. Some actually thought Neil Young had sung the track under an alias.
2. **c.** "Sister Golden Hair"
3. **b.** don't give up until you drink from the silver cup
4. **a.** nothing that he didn't already have
5. **b.** it doesn't look good in snow

Animals

1. **c.** the Alan Price Combo (Alan Price was keyboardist for the original Animals)

2. **b.** War
3. **a.** reach the sky
4. **b.** rags
5. **b.** wear that ball and chain

Association

1. **a.** "Windy" (number one for four weeks in 1967)
2. **c.** the Aristocrats (according to leader Terry Kirkman)
3. **a.** perish
4. **b.** stormy
5. **b.** spend your whole life with them

Bachman-Turner Overdrive

1. **a.** Canada
2. **c.** the Guess Who (Randy Bachman, lead guitarist)
3. **b.** work at nothing
4. **c.** any love is good love
5. **c.** the light

Bad Company

1. **b.** a 1972 movie, starring Jeff Bridges
2. **c.** Swan Song, owned by Led Zeppelin
3. **a.** the Guess Who
4. **a.** a rising sun
5. **b.** your love

Badfinger

1. **b.** Paul McCartney (it appeared in the film *The Magic Christian*)
2. **b.** George Harrison ("Day After Day"), Todd Rundgren ("Baby Blue")
3. **c.** the special love they had for her
4. **a.** their love
5. **a.** money

Beach Boys

1. **b.** the Surfers
2. **a.** David Marks (a neighbor of the Hawthorne, California, band)
3. **a.** "I Get Around" (1964)
4. **a.** "Be True to Your School" (featuring the Honeys)
5. **c.** Glen Campbell
6. **b.** "Surfin' U.S.A." (adapted from Berry's "Sweet Little Sixteen")
7. **c.** Peru
8. **c.** she let another guy come between them
9. **a.** their chick
10. **a.** drive

Beatles

1. **c.** Brian Epstein
2. **c.** the Cavern Club (as the Quarrymen—Paul McCartney had not yet joined and did not perform)
3. **b.** the Beatmakers
4. **b.** Stu Sutcliffe (bass guitarist)
5. **a.** *The Ed Sullivan Show* (February 9, 1964)
6. **c.** "I Want to Hold Your Hand" (seven weeks number one in January 1964)
7. **b.** he was stricken with tonsillitis
8. **c.** David Jones (later singer in the Monkees; he appeared as part of the Broadway musical cast of *Oliver*)
9. **c.** four asteroids (discovered in 1983 and 1984 and named for the Beatles)
10. **c.** happy
11. **a.** reason with you
12. **a.** that she's theirs
13. **a.** the world
14. **a.** not to step on their shoes
15. **a.** Miami

16. **c.** a state of mind
17. **a.** you can count them out
18. **a.** Tucson
19. **c.** hard to see
20. **c.** love

Blondie

1. **c.** Wind in the Willows (from a book by Kenneth Graham)
2. **a.** "Call Me" (number one for six weeks)
3. **c.** your number one
4. **b.** there's no peace of mind
5. **b.** he eats your head

Boston

1. **b.** the members were all from Boston
2. **b.** MIT (a master's degree in mechanical engineering!)
3. **a.** "Amanda"
4. **a.** when they hear the that old song being played
5. **a.** getting behind

David Bowie

1. **a.** the Lower Third
2. **b.** there already was a Davy Jones (with the Monkees)
3. **b.** "Fame"
4. **c.** he often wore dresses
5. **c.** Bing Crosby (in the medley "Peace on Earth"/"Little Drummer Boy")

Jackson Browne

1. **a.** "Somebody's Baby" (from the soundtrack of *Fast Times at Ridgemont High*; it reached number seven)
2. **a.** "Take It Easy"

3. **b.** that it's later than it seems
4. **b.** he's running behind
5. **c.** he's going to make her his tonight

Buckinghams

1. **a.** "Kind of a Drag" (released on the U.S.A. label)
2. **b.** the Pulsations
3. **a.** running around with other guys
4. **a.** their minds
5. **b.** when your baby doesn't love you

Buffalo Springfield

1. **c.** a steamroller (a sign on it read "Buffalo, Springfield")
2. **a.** the Flying Burrito Brothers
3. **a.** David Crosby (he filled in for Neil Young, who had briefly quit the group at that time)
4. **b.** everybody's wrong
5. **c.** because they love you

Byrds

1. **b.** so as not to be confused with "birds," a British slang for "girls"
2. **c.** the Mugwumps
3. **a.** "My Back Pages" (which reached number thirty in 1967)
4. **b.** David Crosby (of Crosby, Stills and Nash; Hillman's Souther-Hillman-Furay band was not highly successful)
5. **c.** an electric guitar

Cheap Trick

1. **b.** Chicken Funk
2. **c.** Rockford, Illinois

3. **b.** Japan
4. **b.** "The Flame" (in 1988)
5. **a.** inside their brain

Chicago

1. **c.** they were threatened with a lawsuit (from the Chicago Transit Authority and Chicago mayor Richard Daley)
2. **c.** each was numbered (from Chicago III to Chicago 19)
3. **b.** Peter Cetera ("Glory of Love" and "The Next Time I Fall," with Amy Grant)
4. **c.** splash their face
5. **b.** they seem like yesterday

Eric Clapton

1. **a.** the Yardbirds
2. **c.** "I Shot the Sheriff" (written by Bob Marley)
3. **a.** having you stay there with him
4. **a.** your tambourine
5. **c.** on their knees

Dave Clark Five

1. **a.** Mike Smith (Dave Clark was the drummer)
2. **a.** "Over and Over"
3. **b.** since you left them
4. **c.** a long time
5. **a.** because they love you

Joe Cocker

1. **b.** Mad Dogs and Englishmen
2. **c.** Woodstock/Woodstock + 25
3. **b.** Ray Charles's piano-playing style (Joe Cocker is *not* spastic.)

4. **c.** not too good
5. **c.** what used to be

Cream

1. **c.** because they considered themselves the "cream of the crop" of British blues players
2. **a.** "While My Guitar Gently Weeps" (from the *White Album*)
3. **b.** what's inside of you
4. **b.** the tired eyes
5. **a.** black

Creedance Clearwater Revival

1. **b.** the Golliwogs
2. **a.** Olympia (from the clear water, used from making it)
3. **a.** a hurricane
4. **a.** a year
5. **a.** high heels

Crosby, Stills and Nash (and Young)

1. **c.** Byrds/Buffalo Springfield/Hollies (Byrds—Crosby; Buffalo Springfield—Stills and Young; Hollies—Nash)
2. **c.** four
3. **b.** your dreams
4. **a.** the water
5. **a.** they turned into butterflies

Deep Purple

1. **b.** a 1963 hit song by Nino Tempo and April Stevens
2. **c.** Vanilla Fudge (whose first Top Forty hit charted only a month before their first hit, "Hush")
3. **b.** Frank Zappa and the Mothers at Montreaux
4. **c.** calling their name
5. **c.** a river

Dire Straits

1. **b.** social worker
2. **a.** Sting (who interjected the melody of "Don't Stand So Close to Me" to the words "I want my MTV")
3. **c.** Talking Heads
4. **b.** singing the oldies
5. **c.** he's got a daytime job

Doobie Brothers

1. **a.** a joint (at the time the name was suggested, the band didn't know of the drug context)
2. **a.** "What a Fool Believes" (number one for one week in 1979)
3. **c.** a way to make them smile
4. **b.** San Antonio
5. **a.** your brother

Doors

1. **a.** *The Doors of Perception* (Aldous Huxley's book, in which "doors" are equated with drugs)
2. **a.** "girl, we couldn't get much higher" (Jim Morrison sang the original line, and the Doors never appeared on *The Ed Sullivan Show* again!)
3. **c.** he exposed himself on stage
4. **a.** a killer
5. **a.** when you're unwanted

Bob Dylan

1. **b.** Robert (Allan) Zimmerman
2. **a.** Woody Guthrie
3. **a.** a motorcycle accident in 1966
4. **a.** they'll sink like a stone
5. **c.** they'll die soon

Eagles

1. **b.** the Byrds
2. **c.** America
3. **a.** "Hotel California"
4. **c.** a mission bell
5. **b.** what a woman can do to your soul

Electric Light Orchestra

1. **c.** "Do Ya" (which reached number twenty-four in 1977)
2. **c.** *Xanadu* (ELO backed Olivia Newton-John on the soundtrack hit)
3. **a.** sailing away on the crest of a wave
4. **a.** get on board the very next train
5. **b.** they do

Emerson, Lake and Palmer

1. **c.** King Crimson
2. **b.** Asia
3. **a.** it doesn't make sense
4. **b.** Have you ever wondered why?
5. **b.** a gold-covered mattress

Fleetwood Mac

1. **c.** John Mayall's Bluesbreakers
2. **a.** "Dreams" (number one for one week in 1977)
3. **b.** "Don't Stop"
4. **c.** drown
5. **a.** you'll see things in a different way

Foreigner

1. **c.** because the members were from both the U.S. and England

2. **b.** Junior Walker (formerly of "Shotgun" fame)
3. **c.** "Waiting for a Girl Like You" (which got upstaged by Olivia Newton-John's "Physical" for most of its reign in 1981)
4. **c.** heartache and pain
5. **a.** your love for them

Peter Frampton

1. **a.** the Herd and Humble Pie
2. **b.** Frampton's Camel
3. **a.** *Frampton Comes Alive*
4. **a.** the sea
5. **c.** your love won't wait

Genesis

1. **a.** Jonathan King (who wrote and sang "Everyone's Gone to the Moon" in 1965 and considered Genesis a fitting name for both the band's—and his own—recent entre into the music business)
2. **b.** Peter Gabriel
3. **b.** he responded to a music magazine ad (in *Melody Maker*, seeking a drummer for the band)
4. **c.** Mike + the Mechanics
5. **c.** you're never quite the same

Grand Funk (Railroad)

1. **a.** the Grand Trunk Railroad
2. **b.** Todd Rundgren
3. **b.** "The Loco-Motion" (number one in 1962 for Little Eva.)
4. **c.** return them their ship
5. **a.** a little bit of rhythm and a lot of soul

Grass Roots

1. **b.** "Midnight Confessions" (number five in 1969)

2. **a.** sad
3. **b.** their soul
4. **b.** dreams that can't come true
5. **c.** love is gonna get you

Grateful Dead

1. **c.** the Warlocks
2. **b.** Fillmore West (in San Francisco—produced by Bill Graham)
3. **c.** experimentation with LSD
4. **a.** Ashbury (in a communal setting at 710 Ashbury Street)
5. **a.** "Touch of Grey"

Guess Who

1. **b.** Chad Allan and the Expressions (Chad Allan sang lead vocals on the track)
2. **a.** they've come and gone
3. **a.** cry
4. **a.** growing old with her
5. **c.** distant roads

Daryl Hall and John Oates

1. **a.** the Everly Brothers
2. **a.** "Maneater" (for four weeks in 1982)
3. **b.** time out
4. **c.** to hide away
5. **b.** until tomorrow

Heart

1. **b.** White Heart
2. **a.** Mike Reno (Loverboy lead singer; in "Almost Paradise," the love theme from *Footloose*)
3. **a.** you're going to burn to the wick

4. **c.** the ticking of the clock
5. **c.** to come home

Jimi Hendrix

1. **a.** the Monkees (Jimi and his group were soon dropped from the billing)
2. **a.** he set his guitar on fire in a bizarre ritual
3. **c.** "All Along the Watchtower" (which reached number twenty in 1968)
4. **a.** that there must be some way out of here
5. **b.** the end of time

Herman's Hermits

1. **b.** leader Peter Noone resembled googly-eyed Sherman on *The Bullwinkle Show*. The group grew out of that to become Herman and His Hermits, later Herman's Hermits....Sherman's Shermits wouldn't have worked as well!
2. **a.** Jimmy Page
3. **b.** *When the Boys Meet the Girls*
4. **a.** 1911
5. **a.** Sam

Hollies

1. **b.** they were inspired by Buddy Holly (some say they were named for the Christmas Season, but Graham Nash set the record straight in a foreword he wrote in 1984)
2. **a.** "Bus Stop" (Though "Look Through Any Window" was their first release that broke into the U.S. charts, it was nowhere near being called a "hit.")
3. **c.** cymbals
4. **a.** janitor
5. **c.** as if they were both quite insane

Tommy James and the Shondells

1. **c.** during study hall in the seventh grade
2. **c.** the Mutual of New York building (Unable to put the right words to an instrumental track, he got the idea of "Mony" as he looked out his window and saw a sign with those now-famous words. He abbreviated them and turned the letters into gold.)
3. **c.** the sun
4. **c.** behave
5. **b.** love her

Jan and Dean

1. **c.** Jennie Lee was a stripper; Arnie (Ginsburg) was a friend (and early group member)
2. **c.** Linda Eastman (now better known as Linda McCartney)
3. **c.** "Barbara Ann" (Dean Torrence walked into the Beach Boys' studio during a break, suggested the song, and then joined the group during the *Beach Boy's Party* album's recording. Due to label conflicts, Dean was not credited for his lead vocals.)
4. **a.** "Surf City" (in 1963)
5. **c.** he got his draft notice

Jefferson Airplane

1. **a.** it was the name of a friend's dog (It is also slang for a marijuana roach-clip, but the group credits four-legged Thomas Jefferson Airplane as their inspiration. After all, a dog—not a joint—is man's best friend. PS: The slang term was derived from the reputation the group had acquired...however, the dog came first, the reputation followed.)
2. **c.** the Great Society
3. **c.** Jefferson Starship and Starship

4. **b.** Haight and Ashbury
5. **a.** nothing

Jethro Tull

1. **b.** an eighteenth-century agriculturalist who invented the seed drill
2. **b.** he often plays while standing on one foot
3. **b.** on a park bench
4. **a.** the monkeys
5. **a.** shout of war's disaster

Elton John

1. **b.** Reginald Dwight
2. **b.** Long John Baldry (the first name came from Baldry's saxophonist, Elton Dean)
3. **c.** Marilyn Monroe
4. **b.** the Pinball Wizard
5. **c.** he waved the flag

Journey

1. **c.** San Francisco
2. **c.** "I Love Rock 'N Roll" (by Joan Jett and the Black-hearts, which spent seven weeks on top in 1982)
3. **a.** How could it be so blind?
4. **b.** when they're all alone
5. **a.** hold on to that feeling

Kinks

1. **c.** the Ravens
2. **c.** "it tastes just like Coca-Cola" changed to "cherry cola." (Coca-Cola threatened the group with a lawsuit due to the overtly sexual nature of the lyrics,

which made it less than a suitable association for the pop drink.)
3. **c.** punctuality
4. **b.** when they're by your side
5. **a.** a lonely soul

Kiss

1. **a.** Israel
2. **b.** each released a solo album (dressed up in Kiss attire)
3. **c.** *Lick It Up*
4. **c.** magic
5. **b.** she's young and clean

Billy J. Kramer and the Dakotas

1. **c.** Brian Epstein (manager of the Beatles)
2. **a.** the Coasters (a local British band—not the American R and B group!)
3. **a.** John Lennon and Paul McCartney (who wrote "Bad to Me," "I'll Keep You Satisfied," and "From a Window")
4. **b.** they're together with their girlfriend
5. **c.** kiss you

Led Zeppelin

1. **a.** the Who (members Keith Moon and John Entwistle, who thought that a supergroup with members like Page and Winwood would flop like a lead balloon—hence, Led Zeppelin)
2. **b.** *Don Kirschner's Rock Concert* (in which they played "Black Dog")
3. **b.** Swan Song
4. **c.** "Stairway to Heaven" (from *Led Zeppelin 4*)
5. **a.** a backdoor man

John Lennon

1. **c.** *Two Virgins*
2. **a.** "Woman"
3. **a.** living life in peace
4. **a.** a superstar
5. **b.** the little child inside the man

Gary Lewis and the Playboys

1. **b.** when Gary Lewis was drafted (in January 1967)
2. **c.** let the stars get in your eyes
3. **a.** count them out
4. **a.** if there's love behind it
5. **a.** they love you

Lovin' Spoonful

1. **c.** the Mamas and the Papas (John Sebastian and Zal Yanovsky teamed with Cass Elliot and Denny Doherty as the Mugwumps, in 1964.)
2. **c.** *You're a Big Boy Now*
3. **b.** *Welcome Back, Kotter*
4. **a.** they would have liked you anyway
5. **b.** a kitty

Lynyrd Skynyrd

1. **b.** They named themselves after a gym teacher who didn't like long-haired students. Leonard Skinner actually introduced the band at a local concert years later, which goes to show that rock and roll leaves no hard feelings!
2. **b.** Neil Young (to whom they sang—in response to Young's attack on the "Southern Man"—that the "Southern man don't need him around anyhow")
3. **a.** *Street Survivors* (the cover of which was changed shortly after the fatal incident)

4. **a.** Would you still remember them
5. **c.** Boise

The Mamas and the Papas

1. **b.** a waitress
2. **a.** "Creeque Alley"
3. **b.** "Monday, Monday"
4. **a.** send her somewhere she's never been
5. **b.** pray

Manfred Mann

1. **c.** Paul Jones (Manfred Mann was the keyboardist)
2. **c.** "The Mighty Quinn"
3. **c.** "Blinded by the Light"
4. **b.** they kissed a little more
5. **a.** in despair

Paul McCartney (and Wings)

1. **a.** "Live and Let Die"
2. **a.** McCartney's pet (a Labrador pup)
3. **c.** "Go Now" (as lead singer for the original Moody Blues)
4. **b.** "Linda" (written by a friend of the Eastman family for Linda Eastman McCartney. The song reached the Top Forty charts for Jan and Dean in 1963.)
5. **a.** "Ebony and Ivory" (with Stevie Wonder, number one for seven weeks, one more than "Say Say Say," his duet with Michael Jackson)

John Cougar Mellencamp

1. **c.** David Bowie (whose manager, Tony DeFries, was contacted by John Mellencamp—a long time fan of David Bowie. DeFries suggested the name Johnny Cougar, though he added his true last name—

Mellencamp—in 1983.)
2. **b.** "Jack and Diane" (number one for four weeks in 1982)
3. **c.** those young boy days
4. **c.** when she got too close to her expectations
5. **a.** in the heartland of America

Men at Work

1. **c.** Australia
2. **c.** the Monkees (with their 1967 album *The Monkees*)
3. **a.** "Overkill"
4. **c.** go away and don't come around there anymore
5. **b.** 6′4″

Steve Miller Band

1. **c.** Les Paul
2. **c.** Boz Scaggs
3. **a.** El Paso
4. **b.** they heat up like a burning flame
5. **c.** 707

Monkees

1. **c.** *Daily Variety*
2. **a.** Glen Campbell (others who *did* apply included Stephen Stills, Paul Williams and Danny Hutton, a founder of Three Dog Night...also, believe it or not, Charles Manson auditioned!)
3. **b.** *Oliver* (he was the Artful Dodger)
4. **c.** *Circus Boy* (as Mickey Braddock)
5. **c.** they're too busy singing to put anybody down

Moody Blues

1. **a.** "Go Now"
2. **a.** Threshold

3. **c.** "Nights in White Satin"
4. **a.** the universe
5. **c.** the fire that is burning

Van Morrison

1. **b.** Northern Ireland
2. **b.** "Gloria" (recorded as "Them")
3. **b.** down in the hollow
4. **a.** a change
5. **a.** make romance

Tom Petty and the Heartbreakers

1. **b.** *Follow That Dream* (starring Elvis Presley and filmed near Tom Petty's home while he was a youngster)
2. **c.** "Don't Do Me Like That"
3. **a.** Bob Dylan
4. **b.** hopeless
5. **b.** somebody must have kicked you around

Pink Floyd

1. **b.** after two blues singers—Pink Anderson and Floyd Council
2. **a.** 1966
3. **a.** "Money"
4. **b.** *Zabriskie Point*
5. **b.** *Dark Side of the Moon* (which has sold more than 13 million copies)

Police

1. **b.** Stewart Copeland's father (who worked in the CIA and taught him the "tricks of the trade")
2. **b.** a favorite black and yellow jersey
3. **a.** *Syncronicity*, which included the single "Every

Breath You Take," number one for eight weeks
4. **c.** Wrigley's gum (they appeared in a Wrigley's chewing gum ad)
5. **c.** since you've gone

Pretenders

1. **b.** from the fifties hit "The Great Pretender"
2. **b.** *The King of Comedy*
3. **b.** a picture of you
4. **b.** your attention
5. **c.** find them

Procol Harum

1. **c.** a friend's Siamese cat (In Latin, the words actually mean "beyond these things," for what it's worth!)
2. **c.** Best British Pop Single 1952–77 award (shared with Queen's "Bohemian Rhapsody")
3. **c.** "Sleepers Awake" (a cantata by Bach)
4. **c.** turn cartwheels
5. **a.** a place to unwind

Gary Puckett and the Union Gap

1. **c.** Bob Dylan (who attended Hibbing High School)
2. **c.** Washington (near where leader Gary Puckett grew up)
3. **b.** Have you got cheating on your mind?
4. **b.** live
5. **b.** sleep

Queen

1. **b.** Tanzania (as Frederick Bulsara)
2. **c.** "Another One Bites the Dust"
3. **a.** *Flash Gordon*
4. **b.** as easy come, easy go

5. a. the world

REO Speedwagon

1. b. the father of the Oldsmobile Corporation (and builder of the fire truck with the group's namesake)
2. c. their eleventh (Formed in 1968, the band titled their tenth album *A Decade of Rock 'n' Roll,* and it featured ten years of their music! Overnight success doesn't always come early!)
3. a. "Can't Fight This Feeling" (which topped the charts for three weeks in 1985)
4. b. there was something missing
5. c. for you to be around

Paul Revere and the Raiders

1. c. Mark Lindsay (Paul Revere was the keyboardist)
2. c. *Happening '68* (*Where The Action Is* began in 1965)
3. b. "Indian Reservation" (number one for one week in 1974)
4. a. have them stay there tonight
5. c. live and die

Rolling Stones

1. b. Brian Jones
2. a. Blues Incorporated
3. c. *The Les Crane Show* (June 2, 1964)
4. c. "Miss You" (in 1978)
5. c. *Rock and Roll Circus*
6. c. "Cocksucker Blues"
7. c. Altamont (a gun-waving fan was killed during the 1969 California concert)
8. b. *Performance*
9. c. *Their Satanic Majesties Request*
10. b. summer

11. **a.** they're still going to miss her
12. **a.** she never listens to their advice
13. **b.** look at someone else
14. **a.** in St. John's Wood
15. **b.** the moon
16. **c.** love that's love
17. **a.** open your eyes
18. **c.** real love
19. **a.** no one can say they didn't try
20. **a.** cry

Mitch Ryder and the Detroit Wheels

1. **b.** Billy Lee and the Rivieras
2. **a.** William Levise Jr. (the name Mitch Ryder was selected from a telephone directory!)
3. **b.** "Linda Sue Dixon"
4. **b.** in the fall
5. **a.** Molly

Searchers

1. **a.** a 1956 movie starring John Wayne
2. **b.** Ringo Starr (who made the switch to replace recently fired Pete Best in another popular local band: the Beatles)
3. **a.** Sonny Bono
4. **b.** seven
5. **a.** get down on her knees

Bob Seger (and The Silver Bullet Band)

1. **b.** Bob Seger System
2. **a.** Del Shannon
3. **c.** *Against the Wind*
4. **a.** the same soul
5. **a.** running

Bruce Springsteen

1. **b.** the E Street Band
2. **b.** "Dancing in the Dark" (number two for four weeks)
3. **c.** Chrysler (which sought "Born in the U.S.A." for their commercials)
4. **c.** the Boss
5. **a.** "Island Girl"/Elton John
6. **c.** Gary U.S. Bonds
7. **b.** spend half your life covering it up
8. **c.** eight
9. **c.** tramps
10. **c.** he never went back

Steely Dan

1. **c.** Through an ad in the *Village Voice*, placed there by guitarist Denny Dias, seeking jazz-oriented rockers. Their original drummer was Chevy Chase, who changed professions and made his claim to fame in comedy!
2. **c.** Jay and the Americans
3. **c.** a steam-powered dildo (as featured in William Burroughs's novel *Naked Lunch*)
4. **b.** the Soul Survivors
5. **c.** saxophone

Steppenwolf

1. **c.** a novel by Herman Hesse
2. **c.** *Candy* and *Easy Rider* (each of which also included songs by the Byrds)
3. **c.** "Born to Be Wild"
4. **c.** the fantasy
5. **a.** tombstones in their eyes

Rod Stewart

1. **a.** the Hollies
2. **a.** soccer
3. **a.** "Tonight's the Night (Gonna Be Alright)" because of its seductive, deflowering lyrics
4. **b.** that time is on their side
5. **c.** September

Supertramp

1. **b.** the 1910 book *The Autobiography of a Supertramp*, by W. H. Davies
2. **b.** a young Dutch millionaire, Stanley Miesegaes
3. **c.** "The Logical Song" (which reached number six in 1979)
4. **b.** your paradise
5. **b.** a wonderful miracle

10cc

1. **a.** Genesis
2. **c.** Wayne Fontana and the Mindbenders (10cc coleader Graham Gouldman also joined the group after Fontana had left—they were then known simply as the Mindbenders.)
3. **c.** "Neanderthal Man" (as Hotlegs)
4. **a.** they're falling in the river
5. **c.** it's just a phase they're going through

Three Dog Night

1. **c.** it's an Australian term for a very cold night (in which one needs three dogs to supply the needed warmth while outdoors)
2. **a.** the Monkees
3. **c.** Hoyt Axton (country singer and writer)

4. b. their trouble and pain
5. c. two

Toto

1. c. It did not come from lead singer Bobby Kimball's last name, Toteaux. *Toto* (a name selected after two members viewed the classic Judy Garland film—which also features Toto, her dog) means "everything" in Latin, is part of a betting term—*Toto Lotto*—in Europe, is a cartoon character in France, and is a large toilet manufacturer in Japan. So it means just about anything. But Bobby Kimball's last name is and always has been Kimball, despite "Toteaux" rumors!)
2. b. "Ironside"
3. c. six (including record and album of the year)
4. a. hold her tight
5. c. drums

Troggs

1. a. a mythical caveman (similar to the "missing link" of evolutionary research)
2. c. England
3. b. fingers and toes
4. a. to spend their life with you
5. c. groovy

Turtles

1. b. the Undivided Sum
2. b. Tyrtles, to imitate the Byrds' spelling
3. a. White Whale
4. c. *200 Motels* (a Frank Zappa film)
5. a. away from their window

Van Halen

1. **a.** Holland
2. **c.** Sammy Hagar (lead singer of lesser-known eighties band Montrose)
3. **a.** Michael Jackson (in the number one song "Beat It")
4. **b.** Valerie Bertinelli
5. **b.** love in the third degree

Who

1. **c.** "High Numbers" sounded too much like gambling (The term actually meant "being in style," but for promotional purposes, it came off more as an ad for bingo than for a rock group.)
2. **c.** smashing their guitars
3. **c.** the Beatles' *All You Need Is Love*, part of a satellite TV-airing
4. **a.** *The Kids Are Alright*
5. **a.** Mama Cass Elliot (of the Mamas and the Papas)

Edgar Winter Group

1. **a.** White Trash
2. **c.** he is albino (as is his brother Johnny)
3. **a.** Rick Derringer, of "Rock and Roll, Hoochie Koo" fame
4. **b.** "Frankenstein," an instrumental whose title came from the extensive editing and reconstruction done to the originally recorded version. It turned into a monster!
5. **c.** lead you to the Promised Land

Yardbirds

1. **a.** Pete Townshend
2. **b.** the New Yardbirds
3. **a.** Will they be bolder than today?

4. **b.** Where is she?
5. **a.** the sun

Young Rascals

1. **b.** Joey Dee and the Starliters (all except Dino Danelli)
2. **b.** "I Ain't Gonna Eat Out My Heart Anymore" (which reached number fifty-two in 1966)
3. **c.** Shea Stadium (as an opening act for the Beatles' New York sellout)
4. **a.** "People Got to Be Free" (number one for five weeks …"Groovin'" was number one for four weeks)
5. **b.** ecstasy

Frank Zappa

1. **c.** Baltimore, Maryland
2. **c.** the Mothers of Invention
3. **c.** Howard Kaylan and Mark Volman (formerly lead singers of the Turtles and prior to their Flo and Eddie fame)
4. **c.** *200 Motels*
5. **c.** "Smoke on the Water" (by Deep Purple)

Zombies

1. **c.** England
2. **b.** 1967 (It was released in 1969, when "the time was right." Oddly, the group had already disbanded, way back in 1967!)
3. **c.** Rod Argent (the song was "Hold Your Head Up")
4. **a.** clear and bright
5. **a.** lovin'

ZZ Top

1. **b.** Texas blues singer Z. Z. Hill
2. **b.** the Moving Sidewalks, who opened for the Jimi

Hendrix Experience in a 1968 concert
3. **b.** Texas
4. **c.** Frank Beard
5. **c.** On October 10, 1987, ZZ Top announced that they'd made an advance booking for the first passenger flight to the moon.

Across the Charts: Classic Rock Artist Trivia

1. **a.** Bob Dylan
2. **c.** the Classics IV
3. **c.** because of reportedly obscene lyrics (One explanation of the lyric's cryptic nature is that they were adapted from Jamaican English, thereby creating variations on the standard pronunciation and making very ordinary lyrics sound unusual, and hence perhaps "obscene" in a subliminal way. However, obscene or not, fact is that the lyrics have never really been understandable, by American or Jamaican audiences!)
4. **c.** William Broad
5. **b.** the Thin White Duke
6. **a.** Fillmore West (1968) and Woodstock (1969)
7. **b.** Roger Daltrey (lead singer of the Who)
8. **b.** *Rocky III*
9. **c.** "de-evolution" (the band's commentary on the status of mankind)
10. **c.** Rick Derringer (born Rick Zehringer)
11. **b.** Bongo and Jawaka
12. **c.** New York
13. **a.** Vincent Damon Furnier
14. **a.** "You Keep Me Hangin' On" (number six in 1968)
15. **b.** Aerosmith
16. **c.** *General Hospital* (he played Noah Drake)
17. **a.** A Vietnam veteran. Writer Bernie Taupin was inspired by an article in *Newsweek* and wrote a tribute to the man it described as fleeing from the lingering memories of the war.
18. **c.** *Back to the Future Part III*

19. **c.** the Amboy Dukes (who recorded "Journey to the Center of the Mind" in 1968)
20. **b.** Big Star
21. **a.** 1964
22. **b.** the Whiskey A-Go-Go
23. **a.** dexedrine, a widely used upper
24. **b.** Climax (who charted with "Precious and Few" in 1972)
25. **c.** "Burning Heart"
26. **a.** "Oye Como Va"
27. **c.** the Nazz (Todd Rundgren's already-named group Nazz had no affiliation with Cooper)
28. **a.** Altamont
29. **a.** Generation X (from 1977 to 1981)
30. **c.** they were all from Kansas
31. **c.** the Ventures ("The McCoy" was the flip of "Walk Don't Run")
32. **c.** *Rolling Stone*'s "Best New Band of the Year"
33. **b.** John Lennon, as a tribute
34. **b.** "Hello It's Me"
35. **a.** Altamont (where a belligerent fan was killed during the Stones' performance)
36. **c.** San Francisco (1964)
37. **b.** Capricorn
38. **a.** Leitch
39. **c.** Outsiders
40. **c.** "Valley Girl" (featuring daughter Moon Unit)
41. **a.** hunting
42. **c.** the USA. (The Ö was added for international appeal.)
43. **a.** to avoid confusion with the group the Trade Winds (they were originally called the Tradewinds when they formed in 1964, but with the 1965 hit "New York's a Lonely Town," by the New York group the Trade Winds, they elected to avoid any possible

future confusion.)

44. c. "Vehicle"/Ides of March (featuring Survivor keyboardist Jim Peterik as lead singer)

45. a. "Mony Mony" (a remake of Tommy James and the Shondells' 1968 hit)

46. b. *Music From Big Pink*

47. c. A suicide attempt by Elton John, brought on by second thoughts and ensuing depression regarding a forthcoming marriage. The marriage plans were terminated, the song became a testimonial and a hit, and Elton John lives on—thank goodness!

48. a. UNICEF (in 1978)

49. c. the Atlanta International Pop Festival

50. a. the Jeff Beck Group

Doo Doo Doo, Da Da Da: Classic Rock Lyrics Questions

Easy as A-B-C

1. **a.** cobblestone
2. **b.** it's a song
3. **a.** wine
4. **b.** dance
5. **a.** a Jaguar
6. **c.** brass
7. **c.** the Mamas and the Papas
8. **c.** anything you desire
9. **c.** Winslow, Arizona
10. **b.** confusion
11. **c.** what a long strange trip it's been
12. **b.** that there's no country
13. **a.** it's his and yours to see
14. **c.** put her down
15. **a.** gray
16. **a.** love
17. **b.** Casablanca
18. **b.** her love belongs to them
19. **c.** they'll hitch a ride
20. **b.** that she couldn't live without them
21. **c.** the Eastern world
22. **c.** funny inside
23. **b.** leave him
24. **a.** Spider Murphy
25. **a.** get used to it
26. **a.** that their eyes still see
27. **b.** a king, clown, or poet

28. **b.** you're not to blame
29. **c.** you'll lose your mind
30. **c.** two weeks
31. **c.** a song and a smile
32. **b.** his hi-fi
33. **c.** money
34. **a.** when the rooster crows
35. **b.** in a girlie magazine
36. **a.** beg them
37. **c.** the way she moves
38. **b.** the dove
39. **a.** a summer shower
40. **c.** a hundred
41. **b.** love you
42. **b.** sixteen
43. **c.** hot and cold fever
44. **b.** that sunny day
45. **b.** nine days
46. **c.** playing with their own ding-a-ling
47. **c.** his clothes
48. **a.** a lonely street
49. **c.** saying goodbye
50. **b.** love you so
51. **c.** 10:00 P.M.
52. **b.** by the record machine
53. **c.** lazin'
54. **b.** because we've gone too far
55. **b.** dance
56. **c.** Zsa Zsa Gabor
57. **a.** raise him back up
58. **b.** Thursdays and Saturdays
59. **a.** New Orleans
60. **a.** one minute
61. **c.** cocaine
62. **b.** if they needed a ride

63. **a.** at the station
64. **a.** life would still go on
65. **a.** take the hand of the man with the lonely eyes
66. **b.** she knows how to use them
67. **a.** fade away
68. **a.** she smiles for the camera
69. **a.** it's like someone's made a six-inch knife cut through the middle of his soul
70. **a.** electric boots and a mohair suit
71. **c.** lighting strikes
72. **b.** his old lady
73. **b.** love has passed them by
74. **c.** forty days
75. **c.** hide
76. **c.** get stoned
77. **c.** pencils, books, and teachers' dirty looks
78. **b.** long blond hair
79. **a.** nothing's wrong
80. **a.** a cloud
81. **a.** leave you
82. **b.** your heart
83. **c.** their love
84. **a.** to the Promised Land
85. **c.** thinking of the future
86. **a.** work
87. **a.** Rita
88. **c.** don't call him
89. **b.** home
90. **c.** an asphalt athlete
91. **c.** 9:00 A.M.
92. **c.** love them
93. **b.** adventure
94. **b.** Detroit
95. **b.** to ease their pain
96. **b.** she'll be back in school

97. **b.** a whiskey bottle
98. **a.** you're not home
99. **a.** in your eyes
100. **b.** just a man and his will to survive

Two Out of Three Ain't Bad

1. **b.** your mama's back
2. **b.** a tough cookie
3. **c.** dreaming of
4. **b.** that he could have her
5. **b.** his brain
6. **a.** a dollar bill
7. **a.** ride them
8. **c.** hurt you
9. **b.** run
10. **b.** Mr. Webster
11. **a.** a chance to hold you in their arms
12. **a.** they're forever banned
13. **c.** 5:00 P.M.
14. **b.** a child of nature and friend of man
15. **b.** in a railroad station
16. **b.** because they had none
17. **a.** a summer's night
18. **c.** you're sitting on top of the world
19. **a.** you're the one they love
20. **a.** take a look at you
21. **a.** sleeping
22. **c.** their father
23. **b.** mourn
24. **c.** pretty
25. **c.** they treat you like you're something new
26. **a.** go out with your fancy friends
27. **c.** for you
28. **c.** the list of the best things in life
29. **a.** their bundle of joy

30. **c.** the trees
31. **a.** the gangster of love
32. **a.** living all their years in a single minute
33. **b.** give her love to them
34. **b.** you took them for everything they had
35. **b.** sing their song
36. **b.** they love her
37. **c.** a super-stock Dodge
38. **b.** a promise
39. **c.** drinking
40. **a.** the day the music died
41. **a.** baby, you're for me
42. **a.** he doesn't need Neil Young around
43. **a.** When will she be his?
44. **a.** Hollywood
45. **b.** walls and minds
46. **a.** the sandman
47. **b.** change their mind
48. **b.** dance
49. **b.** the chance to have you near
50. **c.** mean
51. **b.** show you the way
52. **a.** skyscrapers and freeways
53. **a.** what their heart meant
54. **a.** that you'd be letting him go
55. **c.** getting high all the time
56. **a.** she put a spell on him
57. **b.** provide for you
58. **a.** a midnight fantasy
59. **b.** whether they'll be sure with you
60. **a.** get high
61. **a.** playing baseball
62. **b.** that they're crazy
63. **a.** Mr. Green
64. **c.** hurry a lot

65. **b.** she drops the present she won before
66. **a.** that you're theirs
67. **b.** incomplete
68. **c.** the teacher's pet
69. **b.** peace of mind
70. **c.** make a devil out of them
71. **a.** one long horn
72. **c.** kick off your high-heel sneakers
73. **a.** itch a desire
74. **a.** on the radio
75. **a.** to a movie
76. **c.** it makes you feel good
77. **a.** love
78. **b.** an old fruit jar
79. **c.** happy
80. **b.** take his protein pills and put his helmet on
81. **c.** If he came back, which one would you choose?
82. **b.** a man on a fuzzy tree
83. **a.** her eyes
84. **c.** their world
85. **b.** blue
86. **a.** that they love you
87. **c.** that there's no mountain they can't climb
88. **b.** colorful clothes
89. **a.** a chapel
90. **c.** the sound of T. Rex
91. **c.** the sun
92. **b.** a drunkard's dream
93. **a.** a boy who wants to love only them
94. **a.** frisky
95. **a.** so old they shine
96. **a.** plant your love
97. **a.** you don't learn everything there
98. **c.** wet and naked
99. **a.** Juanita

100. **b.** rainy

Help!

1. **c.** once a week
2. **c.** because you told them so
3. **c.** the bull
4. **c.** tell them your name
5. **a.** Nazareth
6. **c.** older
7. **b.** the guy behind him
8. **a.** they can't understand a single word
9. **a.** with their bones and flesh
10. **a.** get away from you-know-who
11. **a.** one dollar
12. **c.** a secondhand guitar
13. **c.** whether you're letting them in or letting them go
14. **b.** the booze and ladies
15. **c.** a police car
16. **a.** find another girl like you
17. **c.** dreams of the past
18. **a.** ten
19. **b.** calling
20. **b.** education
21. **a.** on the corner
22. **a.** walk on by
23. **c.** because of the dogs
24. **a.** the altar
25. **b.** suppertime
26. **b.** Miss Lucy
27. **a.** a funeral pyre
28. **c.** which way the wind blows
29. **c.** heaven
30. **b.** Will it ruin your reputation?
31. **b.** terrified
32. **c.** pass

33. **b.** go home
34. **a.** everything
35. **c.** Mama Cass
36. **c.** inside four walls
37. **c.** kicking a can
38. **c.** robins and flowers
39. **b.** light their fire
40. **a.** Baton Rouge
41. **a.** she's got no soul
42. **c.** her friends
43. **a.** forget about them
44. **a.** because they'll make their own lightning
45. **c.** it's so unreal
46. **c.** New York City
47. **c.** hold on
48. **b.** your red shoes
49. **c.** another guy
50. **c.** gaze into your eyes
51. **b.** play a tune for them
52. **c.** at Dino's Bar and Grill
53. **c.** around midnight
54. **c.** electrical bananas
55. **b.** you might need it someday
56. **b.** the doctor
57. **a.** keep your love alive
58. **a.** the good Lord will take you away
59. **c.** the beauty did not last
60. **a.** tomorrow
61. **b.** with eyes closed
62. **b.** kissed a woman
63. **a.** tell them lies and cut them down to size
64. **b.** a gas
65. **a.** show how you feel
66. **c.** home
67. **b.** they're the fastest in the nation

68. **a.** Suzie
69. **a.** Frank and Paul
70. **c.** you belong to them
71. **a.** himself
72. **b.** someone to show them
73. **a.** there's a better life for you and them
74. **a.** the hamburger stand
75. **c.** he shot her
76. **c.** chicken
77. **b.** a man from Mars
78. **b.** that they were wrong
79. **a.** they do
80. **a.** they start crying
81. **a.** a young apprentice
82. **c.** the sound of thunder
83. **a.** be there
84. **c.** he commits social suicide
85. **a.** fly
86. **b.** driving
87. **c.** that it feels so right being with them tonight
88. **a.** take it higher
89. **c.** party
90. **c.** falling in love
91. **c.** that you're always there but just don't care
92. **b.** that he'll be holding you close tonight
93. **a.** set her soul on fire
94. **a.** Why must they be a teenager in love?
95. **b.** a wreck
96. **a.** time
97. **a.** money
98. **c.** down by the river
99. **b.** a negligee
100. **b.** the eagle

Hit Me With Your Best Shot

1. **c.** be bad to you
2. **b.** Mr. Hughes
3. **b.** voodoo
4. **c.** because it's never been beat
5. **c.** why you lied to them
6. **a.** a sweet thing
7. **b.** call the state militia
8. **b.** you stood there grinning
9. **c.** you're already attached
10. **c.** come true
11. **c.** Why don't you love clowns?
12. **b.** go
13. **b.** tonight
14. **a.** it's good enough for him
15. **c.** that love is blind
16. **b.** free
17. **c.** by the record machine
18. **a.** as dynamite with a laser beam
19. **c.** at the top of the Ferris wheel
20. **c.** alone
21. **c.** uptight
22. **c.** their heart skips a beat
23. **b.** talk about it
24. **c.** the hand of fate
25. **c.** the land of ice and snow
26. **b.** talk
27. **a.** blow your mind
28. **b.** to the wind
29. **c.** fly
30. **b.** wherever the river flows
31. **a.** they're going to fade away
32. **a.** love
33. **c.** a six-gun in their hand

34. **a.** walk up to her and talk to her
35. **c.** get you
36. **b.** a frustrating mess
37. **b.** they are waiting for a lady to come by
38. **b.** their imagination
39. **b.** nothing except to put a man six feet in a hole
40. **c.** lies
41. **a.** the night they first met you
42. **a.** one night
43. **a.** you were meant to be here
44. **a.** drinking a piña colada
45. **a.** Pasadena
46. **a.** you love him
47. **b.** your love
48. **c.** inside your mind
49. **b.** spend all their money
50. **c.** Jesus freaks
51. **b.** going out
52. **c.** jumping up and down in your blue suede shoes
53. **c.** turning on the heat
54. **b.** a thousand hearts
55. **c.** his china doll in Hong Kong
56. **c.** Hollywood
57. **b.** carnivals and cotton candy
58. **a.** we are only what we feel
59. **c.** Monday
60. **b.** a Mississippi queen
61. **c.** conversation
62. **a.** Huntington Beach
63. **a.** every hung-up person
64. **c.** about an hour ago
65. **a.** fighting back
66. **b.** they dim the lights
67. **c.** the hangman
68. **b.** get burned

69. **c.** in a circle
70. **a.** disappear
71. **b.** it's taken its toll on her
72. **a.** Where do we go from here?
73. **a.** the future
74. **b.** in Dallas and Hollywood
75. **c.** get down on their knees and pray
76. **c.** live and love
77. **a.** your mind
78. **c.** "Love Me Do"
79. **a.** Beatles
80. **c.** an empty shell
81. **a.** in clover
82. **a.** it goes on
83. **b.** because it's so hard to get through to you
84. **c.** if they can't have you to themselves
85. **b.** salivate like a Pavlov dog
86. **c.** juvenile delinquent wrecks
87. **b.** get back to her
88. **a.** put them on a highway and show them a sign
89. **a.** change their life
90. **c.** they don't know her name
91. **b.** complain
92. **a.** the rains
93. **b.** stowing away the time
94. **a.** a death trap
95. **c.** a teeny bopper
96. **a.** a baby's brain and an old man's heart
97. **a.** the blacksmith and the artist
98. **b.** hanging on in quiet desperation
99. **c.** Romeo
100. **b.** believe it if you need it or leave it if you dare

Name That Tune: Classic Rock Title Questions

Take It Easy

1. **b.** "Turn! Turn! Turn!"/Byrds
2. **c.** "Jailhouse Rock"/Elvis Presley
3. **b.** "Black and White"/Three Dog Night
4. **a.** "Whole Lotta Love"/Led Zeppelin
5. **a.** "Smokin' in the Boy's Room"/Brownsville Station
6. **a.** "Proud Mary"/Creedence Clearwater Revival
7. **c.** "Rich Girl"/Daryl Hall and John Oates
8. **a.** "I Shot the Sheriff"/Eric Clapton
9. **c.** "The Lion Sleeps Tonight"/Tokens
10. **b.** "Hotel California"/Eagles
11. **a.** "Every Breath You Take"/Police
12. **b.** "Brown-Eyed Girl"/Van Morrison
13. **c.** "Dust in the Wind"/Kansas
14. **b.** "Shake, Rattle and Roll"/Bill Haley and His Comets
15. **a.** "Oh, Pretty Woman"/Van Halen
16. **c.** "Rikki Don't Lose That Number"/Steely Dan
17. **c.** "Uncle Albert"/Paul and Linda McCartney
18. **a.** "We're an American Band"/Grand Funk Railroad
19. **a.** "Venus"/Bananarama
20. **a.** "Lola"/Kinks
21. **b.** "White Wedding"/Billy Idol
22. **a.** "Jack and Diane"/John Cougar
23. **c.** "Monterey"/Eric Burdon and the Animals
24. **b.** "Another Brick in the Wall"/Pink Floyd
25. **a.** "Last Train to Clarksville"/Monkees
26. **a.** "Like a Rolling Stone"/Bob Dylan
27. **a.** "Hot Blooded"/Foreigner
28. **c.** "California Dreamin'"/The Mamas and the Papas
29. **a.** "Do You Believe in Magic"/Lovin' Spoonful

30. **b.** "Woodstock"/Crosby, Stills, Nash and Young
31. **b.** "Sledgehammer"/Peter Gabriel
32. **a.** "Saturday in the Park"/Chicago
33. **b.** "Bad Moon Rising"/Creedence Clearwater Revival
34. **c.** "Wild Night"/Van Morrison
35. **b.** "Piece of My Heart"/Big Brother and the Holding Company
36. **c.** "She Loves You"/Beatles
37. **c.** "Take It on the Run"/REO Speedwagon
38. **a.** "Woman"/John Lennon
39. **b.** "Easy to Be Hard"/Three Dog Night
40. **b.** "All Shook Up"/Elvis Presley
41. **c.** "More Than a Feeling"/Boston
42. **a.** "The House of the Rising Sun"/Animals
43. **c.** "The Tide Is High"/Blondie
44. **c.** "She's Gone"/Daryl Hall and John Oates
45. **b.** "Money for Nothing"/Dire Straits
46. **c.** "Good Lovin'"/Young Rascals
47. **a.** "My Generation"/Who
48. **c.** "Imagine"/John Lennon
49. **a.** "Ride the Wild Surf"/Jan and Dean
50. **a.** "Stairway to Heaven"/Led Zeppelin
51. **a.** "Tired of Waiting for You"/Kinks
52. **b.** "Live and Let Die"/Wings
53. **c.** "Dance With Me"/Orleans
54. **a.** "Love Is All Around"/Troggs
55. **a.** "Life Is a Rock"/Reunion
56. **a.** "Young Girl"/Gary Puckett and the Union Gap
57. **c.** "Maybe I'm Amazed"/Paul McCartney
58. **c.** "Dancing in the Moonlight"/King Harvest
59. **b.** "Hey Joe"/Jimi Hendrix
60. **a.** "Valleri"/Monkees
61. **a.** "Taking Care of Business"/Bachman-Turner Overdrive
62. **b.** "Windy"/Association

63. **b.** "Your Mama Don't Dance"/Loggins and Messina
64. **b.** "Back in the USSR"/Beatles
65. **c.** "Cecilia"/Simon and Garfunkel
66. **a.** "Born to Be Wild"/Steppenwolf
67. **b.** "Tonight's the Night"/Rod Stewart
68. **a.** "Layla"/Derek and the Dominos
69. **c.** "Traces"/Classics IV
70. **b.** "Take Me Home"/Phil Collins
71. **a.** "Africa"/Toto
72. **a.** "Let's Live for Today"/Grass Roots
73. **c.** "Kentucky Woman"/Neil Diamond
74. **c.** "We Will Rock You"/Queen
75. **b.** "Can't Get Enough"/Bad Company
76. **c.** "Monkees Theme (Hey Hey, We're The Monkees)"/Monkees
77. **c.** "Surfin' Bird"/Trashmen
78. **b.** "Cat Scratch Fever"/Ted Nugent
79. **b.** "American Pie"/Don McLean
80. **b.** "Lyin' Eyes"/Eagles
81. **b.** "Don't Stop"/Fleetwood Mac
82. **b.** "Benny and the Jets"/Elton John
83. **c.** "Day Tripper"/Beatles
84. **c.** "Dawn"/Four Seasons
85. **b.** "Old Days"/Chicago
86. **a.** "I'm Not in Love"/10cc
87. **a.** "Dance to the Music"/Sly and the Family Stone
88. **a.** "Ramblin Man"/Allman Brothers Band
89. **b.** "Goodbye Yellow Brick Road"/Elton John
90. **a.** "Rapture"/Blondie
91. **a.** "You're the Only Woman"/Ambrosia
92. **c.** "Strawberry Fields Forever"/Beatles
93. **a.** "My Woman From Tokyo"/Deep Purple
94. **b.** "Help Me, Rhonda"/Beach Boys
95. **a.** "Silly Love Songs"/Wings
96. **a.** "Summertime Blues"/Eddie Cochran

97. **b.** "Sussudio"/Phil Collins
98. **b.** "Keep on Loving You"/REO Speedwagon
99. **b.** "Rebel Yell"/Billy Idol
100. **c.** "Long Cool Woman"/Hollies

Who Can It Be Now?

1. **c.** "Sister Golden Hair"/America
2. **b.** "Hang On Sloopy"/McCoys
3. **a.** "Venus"/Shocking Blue
4. **c.** "On a Carousel"/Hollies
5. **b.** "Show Me the Way"/Peter Frampton
6. **a.** "Crystal Blue Persuasion"/Tommy James and the Shondells
7. **c.** "Knockin' on Heaven's Door"/Bob Dylan
8. **a.** "With a Little Luck"/Wings
9. **c.** "Hit Me With Your Best Shot"/Pat Benatar
10. **c.** "Long Train Runnin'"/Doobie Brothers
11. **c.** "C. C. Rider"/Mitch Ryder and the Detroit Wheels
12. **b.** "Drive"/Cars
13. **c.** "Heart Full of Soul"/Yardbirds
14. **b.** "Rock and Roll Hoochie Koo"/Rick Derringer
15. **c.** "Can't Buy Me Love"/Beatles
16. **a.** "Imaginary Lover"/Atlanta Rhythm Section
17. **b.** "Bad Case of Loving You"/Robert Palmer
18. **b.** "Watching the Wheels"/John Lennon
19. **b.** "In-A-Gadda-Da-Vida"/Iron Butterfly
20. **c.** "Wasted on the Way"/Crosby, Stills and Nash
21. **a.** "Start Me Up"/Rolling Stones
22. **b.** "It's My Life"/Animals
23. **c.** "Moondance"/Van Morrison
24. **c.** "Refugee"/Tom Petty and the Heartbreakers
25. **c.** "Instant Karma (We All Shine On)"/John Lennon
26. **a.** "Vehicle"/Ides of March
27. **b.** "Memphis"/Johnny Rivers
28. **b.** "Yesterday's Gone"/Chad and Jeremy

29. **b.** "Spill the Wine"/Eric Burdon and War
30. **b.** "I'm a Believer"/Monkees
31. **b.** "Born in the U.S.A."/Bruce Springsteen
32. **c.** "You Can Do Magic"/America
33. **c.** "Can't You See That She's Mine"/Dave Clark Five
34. **a.** "Don't Stand So Close to Me"/Police
35. **c.** "Take the Money and Run"/Steve Miller Band
36. **c.** "Dance With Me"/Orleans
37. **a.** "Take It on the Run"/REO Speedwagon
38. **c.** "Take It to the Limit"/Eagles
39. **c.** "Dreams"/Fleetwood Mac
40. **b.** "Hey Nineteen"/Steely Dan
41. **b.** "Going Up the Country"/Canned Heat
42. **b.** "Dirty Water"/Standells
43. **a.** "Nineteenth Nervous Breakdown"/Rolling Stones
44. **c.** "Joy to the World"/Three Dog Night
45. **b.** "Subterranean Homesick Blues"/Bob Dylan
46. **a.** "How Much I Feel"/Ambrosia
47. **c.** "Ride Captain Ride"/Blues Image
48. **a.** "Dancing in the Dark"/Bruce Springsteen
49. **c.** "Space Oddity"/David Bowie
50. **c.** "Ruby Tuesday"/Rolling Stones
51. **a.** "Eight Miles High"/Byrds
52. **a.** "New Kid in Town"/Eagles
53. **a.** "Whip It"/Devo
54. **c.** "People Got to Be Free"/Rascals
55. **c.** "Walk on the Wild Side"/Lou Reed
56. **b.** "Daydream Believer"/Monkees
57. **c.** "Gloria"/Shadows of Knight
58. **a.** "Surfin' U.S.A."/Beach Boys
59. **c.** "I Just Want to Celebrate"/Rare Earth
60. **b.** "San Francisco (Be Sure to Wear Flowers in Your Hair)"/Scott McKenzie
61. **c.** "A Horse With No Name"/America
62. **a.** "Baby Hold On"/Eddie Money

63. **a.** "Still the One"/Orleans
64. **a.** "Rosanna"/Toto
65. **c.** "Fly Like an Eagle"/Steve Miller Band
66. **b.** "My Sharona"/Knack
67. **a.** "You Baby"/Turtles
68. **b.** "Free Bird"/Lynyrd Skynyrd
69. **b.** "All Right Now"/Free
70. **c.** "Touch of Grey"/Grateful Dead
71. **a.** "Maggie May"/Rod Stewart
72. **c.** "Cry Like a Baby"/Boxtops
73. **b.** "Holdin' On to Yesterday"/Ambrosia
74. **a.** "Love Potion Number Nine"/Searchers
75. **c.** "Come On Eileen"/Dexys Midnight Runners
76. **c.** "Can't Fight This Feeling"/REO Speedwagon
77. **b.** "Listen to What the Man Said"/Wings
78. **c.** "What I Like About You"/Romantics
79. **c.** "Legs"/ZZ Top
80. **b.** "Burning Love"/Elvis Presley
81. **a.** "Oh Sherrie"/Steve Perry
82. **b.** "Two Out of Three Ain't Bad"/Meat Loaf
83. **c.** "Peg"/Steely Dan
84. **c.** "Down Under"/Men at Work
85. **a.** "Another One Bites the Dust"/Queen
86. **c.** "Cold As Ice"/Foreigner
87. **c.** "The Lady in Red"/Chris DeBurgh
88. **a.** "The Things We Do for Love"/10cc
89. **a.** "Pinball Wizard"/Who
90. **c.** "Got My Mind Set on You"/George Harrison
91. **c.** "Shakin' All Over"/Guess Who
92. **b.** "Ferry Cross the Mersey"/Gerry and the Pace-makers
93. **c.** "Abracadabra"/Steve Miller Band
94. **b.** "School Day"/Chuck Berry
95. **b.** "Sunshine of Your Love"/Cream
96. **c.** "Bohemian Rhapsody"/Queen

97. **b.** "Touch Me"/Doors
98. **b.** "You're in My Heart"/Rod Stewart
99. **b.** "Pink Houses"/John Cougar Mellencamp
100. **b.** "Straight On"/Heart

We Don't Need No Education

1. **a.** "Soul Deep"/Boxtops
2. **a.** "One More Night"/Phil Collins
3. **c.** "Born to Run"/Loverboy
4. **a.** "Heartache Tonight"/Eagles
5. **b.** "I'm Into Something Good"/Herman's Hermits
6. **b.** "The Joker"/Steve Miller Band
7. **c.** "Teach Your Children"/Crosby, Stills, Nash and Young
8. **c.** "Who's Crying Now"/Journey
9. **a.** "Bad Company"/Bad Company
10. **b.** "Making Love Out of Nothing At All"/Air Supply
11. **b.** "She's Not There"/Zombies
12. **c.** "Get Together"/Youngbloods
13. **a.** "Kicks"/Paul Revere and the Raiders
14. **a.** "Surf City"/Jan and Dean
15. **c.** "(I'm Not Your) Steppin' Stone"/Monkees
16. **a.** "Casey Jones"/Grateful Dead
17. **b.** "Time Won't Let Me"/Outsiders
18. **c.** "The Letter"/Boxtops
19. **b.** "Mr. Roboto"/Styx
20. **c.** "Living in the U.S.A."/Steve Miller Band
21. **b.** "Say You Love Me"/Fleetwood Mac
22. **b.** "Dream Weaver"/Gary Wright
23. **c.** "Let Your Love Flow"/Bellamy Brothers
24. **b.** "Free Ride"/Edgar Winter Group
25. **c.** "Carrie-Anne"/Hollies
26. **a.** "Strange Brew"/Cream
27. **c.** "Break My Stride"/Matthew Wilder
28. **b.** "Let's Go"/Cars

29. **b.** "Invisible Touch"/Genesis
30. **b.** "Baby I Love Your Way"/Peter Frampton
31. **b.** "Video Killed the Radio Star"/Buggles
32. **a.** "Five O'Clock World"/Vogues
33. **c.** "Sweet Home Alabama"/Lynyrd Skynyrd
34. **b.** "Do It Again"/Steely Dan
35. **a.** "Lost in Love"/Air Supply
36. **a.** "Question"/Moody Blues
37. **a.** "Urgent"/Foreigner
38. **b.** "You Ain't Seen Nothin' Yet"/Bachman-Turner Overdrive
39. **a.** "A Little Bit of Soul"/Music Explosion
40. **b.** "Don't Pay the Ferryman"/Chris De Burgh
41. **c.** "Catch Us If You Can"/Dave Clark Five
42. **c.** "Reason to Believe"/Rod Stewart
43. **b.** "You Might Think"/Cars
44. **a.** "Back on the Chain Gang"/Pretenders
45. **a.** "Go Your Own Way"/Fleetwood Mac
46. **a.** "Fire"/Jimi Hendrix
47. **c.** "I Want You to Want Me"/Cheap Trick
48. **b.** "Middle of the Road"/Pretenders
49. **c.** "Goodbye Stranger"/Supertramp
50. **a.** "I Was Only Joking"/Rod Stewart
51. **a.** "Addicted to Love"/Robert Palmer
52. **c.** "Deacon Blues"/Steely Dan
53. **c.** "Radar Love"/Golden Earring
54. **c.** "Don't Worry Baby"/Beach Boys
55. **b.** "Black Water"/Doobie Brothers
56. **b.** "Maneater"/Daryl Hall and John Oates
57. **c.** "For What It's Worth"/Buffalo Springfield
58. **c.** "Brown Sugar"/Rolling Stones
59. **b.** "Let It Ride"/Bachman-Turner Overdrive
60. **b.** "Philadelphia Freedom"/Elton John Band
61. **b.** "Livin' Thing"/Electric Light Orchestra
62. **c.** "Don't Let Me Be Misunderstood"/Animals

63. **b.** "Eye of the Tiger"/Survivor
64. **b.** "Doo Doo Doo Doo Doo"/Rolling Stones
65. **c.** "Somebody's Baby"/Jackson Browne
66. **a.** "Positively Fourth Street"/Bob Dylan
67. **a.** "I'm a Man"/Spencer Davis Group
68. **c.** "So in to You"/Atlanta Rhythm Section
69. **c.** "One of These Nights"/Eagles
70. **c.** "Who Can It Be Now?"/Men at Work
71. **a.** "Someone Saved My Life Tonight"/Elton John
72. **b.** "96 Tears"/? and the Mysterians
73. **a.** "Hell Is for Children"/Pat Benatar
74. **b.** "Against the Wind"/Bob Seger
75. **a.** "Centerfold"/J. Geils Band
76. **b.** "Come and Get Your Love"/Redbone
77. **a.** "Stop Draggin' My Heart Around"/Stevie Nicks and Tom Petty
78. **a.** "King of Pain"/Police
79. **c.** "Time of the Season"/Zombies
80. **c.** "Old Time Rock and Roll"/Bob Seger and the Silver Bullet Band
81. **c.** "Fool (If You Think It's Over)"/Chris Rea
82. **b.** "Small Town"/John Cougar Mellencamp
83. **b.** "Barbara Ann"/Regents
84. **b.** "Go All the Way"/Raspberries
85. **a.** "Dazed and Confused"/Led Zeppelin
86. **b.** "Barracuda"/Heart
87. **a.** "God"/John Lennon
88. **c.** "Feeling Alright"/Joe Cocker
89. **c.** "Jessie's Girl"/Rick Springfield
90. **a.** "Are You a Boy or Are You a Girl?"/Barbarians
91. **c.** "The Last Time"/Rolling Stones
92. **c.** "The Boys Are Back in Town"/Thin Lizzy
93. **b.** "Don't Stop Believin'"/Journey
94. **b.** "She'd Rather Be With Me"/Turtles
95. **c.** "That's All!"/Genesis

96. **a.** "These Eyes"/Guess Who
97. **a.** "Hush"/Deep Purple
98. **c.** "I Ran (So Far Away)"/A Flock of Seagulls
99. **a.** "Heat of the Moment"/Asia
100. **b.** "Walk of Life"/Dire Straits

Take It to the Limit

1. **c.** "The Love That's Deep Within You"/Moody Blues
2. **a.** "A Whiter Shade of Pale"/Procol Harum
3. **c.** "Girls on Film"/Duran Duran
4. **b.** "Our House"/Crosby, Stills, Nash and Young
5. **a.** "Hold Your Head Up"/Argent
6. **b.** "Brass in Pocket (I'm Special)"/Pretenders
7. **a.** "Crazy on You"/Heart
8. **b.** "Pretty Ballerina"/Left Banke
9. **c.** "More Than a Feeling"/Boston
10. **c.** "Shapes of Things"/Yardbirds
11. **b.** "Stop! Stop! Stop!"/Hollies
12. **c.** "Crocodile Rock"/Elton John
13. **b.** "(Don't Fear) the Reaper"/Blue Öyster Cult
14. **b.** "You Make My Dreams"/Daryl Hall and John Oates
15. **a.** "Lady"/Little River Band
16. **a.** "Break On Through to the Other Side"/Doors
17. **a.** "Goody Two Shoes"/Adam Ant
18. **b.** "My Hometown"/Bruce Springsteen
19. **a.** "Bungle in the Jungle"/Jethro Tull
20. **c.** "Sit Down, I Think I Love You"/Mojo Men
21. **c.** "Crazy Little Thing Called Love"/Queen
22. **c.** "Magic Man"/Heart
23. **c.** "Take the Long Way Home"/Supertramp
24. **b.** "Our Lips Are Sealed"/Go-Go's
25. **c.** "Money"/Pink Floyd
26. **a.** "Tush"/ZZ Top
27. **b.** "Dear Mr. Fantasy"/Traffic
28. **a.** "Sha La La"/Manfred Mann

29. **b.** "Respectable"/Outsiders
30. **a.** "Conquistador"/Procol Harum
31. **b.** "Eye in the Sky"/Alan Parsons Project
32. **a.** "Blue Morning, Blue Day"/Foreigner
33. **a.** "Sooner or Later"/Grass Roots
34. **c.** "Play With Fire"/Rolling Stones
35. **a.** "Nights in White Satin"/Moody Blues
36. **b.** "Nashville Cats"/Lovin' Spoonful
37. **b.** "Hollywood Nights"/Bob Seger and the Silver Bullet Band
38. **b.** "Authority Song"/John Cougar Mellencamp
39. **c.** "Baby Come Back"/Player
40. **c.** "Incense and Peppermints"/Strawberry Alarm Clock
41. **c.** "Evil Woman"/Electric Light Orchestra
42. **a.** "My Back Pages"/Byrds
43. **a.** "Dancing in the Dark"/Bruce Springsteen
44. **b.** "What's Your Name"/Lynyrd Skynyrd
45. **b.** "We Just Disagree"/Dave Mason
46. **c.** "Hello, I Love You"/Doors
47. **a.** "She's About a Mover"/Sir Douglas Quintet
48. **c.** "Sister Christian"/Night Ranger
49. **c.** "Killer Queen"/Queen
50. **c.** "Dream On"/Aerosmith
51. **a.** "Lies"/Knickerbockers
52. **b.** "I Got a Line on You"/Spirit
53. **b.** "Living in the Past"/Jethro Tull
54. **a.** "25 or 6 to 4"/Chicago
55. **b.** "Don't Look Back"/Boston
56. **b.** "Running on Empty"/Jackson Browne
57. **a.** "China Girl"/David Bowie
58. **c.** "Double Shot"/Swingin' Medallions
59. **b.** "Beth"/Kiss
60. **a.** "Temptation Eyes"/Grass Roots
61. **c.** "Biggest Part of Me"/Ambrosia

62. **a.** "Lights"/Journey
63. **c.** "Eyes Without a Face"/Billy Idol
64. **a.** "Liar, Liar"/Castaways
65. **b.** "D'yer Maker"/Led Zeppelin
66. **c.** "In the Air Tonight"/Phil Collins
67. **c.** "Sympathy for the Devil"/Rolling Stones
68. **a.** "Sara"/Fleetwood Mac
69. **b.** "Come Sail Away"/Styx
70. **a.** "Sunny Afternoon"/Kinks
71. **c.** "Games People Play"/Alan Parsons Project
72. **b.** "White Room"/Cream
73. **a.** "Blinded by the Light"/Manfred Mann's Earth Band
74. **c.** "Strange Way"/Firefall
75. **b.** "Blue Jean"/David Bowie
76. **b.** "Conquistador"/Procol Harum
77. **b.** "Ebony Eyes"/Bob Welch
78. **b.** "Head Games"/Foreigner
79. **b.** "Tobacco Road"/Nashville Teens
80. **a.** "On the Way Home"/Buffalo Springfield
81. **b.** "The Logical Song"/Supertramp
82. **b.** "Blowin' in the Wind"/Peter, Paul and Mary
83. **c.** "Anna"/Beatles
84. **b.** "Something in the Air"/Thunderclap Newman
85. **a.** "Lucky Man"/Emerson, Lake and Palmer
86. **b.** "Burnin' for You"/Blue Öyster Cult
87. **a.** "Sugar Mountain"/Neil Young
88. **c.** "Pushin' Too Hard"/Seeds
89. **c.** "Electric Avenue"/Eddy Grant
90. **a.** "1984"/Spirit
91. **b.** "Cruel to Be Kind"/Nick Lowe
92. **a.** "I Was Made for Lovin' You"/Kiss
93. **a.** "Mexican Radio"/Wall of Voodoo
94. **a.** "My Sharona"/Knack
95. **a.** "Call Me"/Blondie
96. **b.** "I Had Too Much to Dream"/Electric Prunes

97. **b.** "Little Girl"/Syndicate of Sound
98. **b.** "Journey to the Center of the Mind"/Amboy Dukes
99. **c.** "Talk, Talk"/Music Machine
100. **c.** "Love Her Madly"/Doors

Rock of Ages: Tomorrow's Classic Rockers

Lyrics

1. **a.** the secrets that you keep
2. **b.** red, gold, and green
3. **a.** walk five hundred more
4. **b.** it opened up their eyes
5. **c.** the magic
6. **b.** frantic
7. **a.** mythical
8. **b.** they get chills
9. **c.** tremble
10. **b.** his Sunday shoes
11. **c.** growing old
12. **a.** through their heart
13. **c.** being stoned
14. **c.** rumors
15. **b.** it's where the grass is green and the girls are pretty
16. **a.** save them
17. **b.** give him attention or affection
18. **c.** stupid and contagious
19. **c.** kill him
20. **a.** touch you
21. **b.** take you in their arms
22. **c.** not so bright
23. **c.** love
24. **a.** turning your back on Mother Nature
25. **c.** Tommy and Gina
26. **a.** pull down the shades
27. **c.** a rodeo

28. **b.** make the girls go crazy
29. **a.** five
30. **b.** you lose the rhythm
31. **c.** leave them behind
32. **c.** in the spaces in between
33. **a.** that she's growing up too fast
34. **b.** lying on the beach and having fun
35. **a.** new bands
36. **b.** motivation
37. **b.** safer
38. **b.** where to look
39. **c.** make mistakes
40. **c.** bow down before the one you serve
41. **a.** Twister and Risk
42. **a.** grey
43. **c.** kneel
44. **b.** the blood on their hands
45. **b.** your hate
46. **a.** voices of friends
47. **c.** confused
48. **b.** that they'll never be in love again
49. **a.** a smile
50. **a.** nuclear science

Titles

1. **c.** "Runaway Train"/Soul Asylum
2. **b.** "Livin' on the Edge"/Aerosmith
3. **c.** "Beds Are Burning"/Midnight Oil
4. **a.** "Creep"/Stone Temple Pilots
5. **b.** "If I Ever Lose My Faith in You"/Sting
6. **c.** "What I Am"/Edie Brickell and New Bohemians
7. **b.** "Losing My Religion"/R.E.M.
8. **a.** "Love is All Around"/Wet Wet Wet
9. **c.** "Under the Bridge"/Red Hot Chili Peppers
10. **a.** "Enjoy the Silence"/Depeche Mode

11. **b.** "No Rain"/Blind Melon
12. **a.** "Everyday"/Phil Collins
13. **b.** "Everybody Have Fun Tonight"/Wang Chung
14. **c.** "The Boys of Summer"/Don Henley
15. **b.** "Your Wildest Dreams"/Moody Blues
16. **b.** "Mary Jane's Last Dance"/Tom Petty and the Heartbreakers
17. **a.** "Enter Sandman"/Metallica
18. **a.** "Make Me Lose Control"/Eric Carmen
19. **c.** "Voices Carry"/'Til Tuesday
20. **c.** "Come As You Are"/Nirvana
21. **b.** "Some Like It Hot"/Power Station
22. **c.** "Mmm Mmm Mmm Mmm"/Crash Test Dummies
23. **a.** "Never Say Goodbye"/Bon Jovi
24. **a.** "She Talks to Angels"/Black Crowes
25. **c.** "Wild, Wild West"/Escape Club
26. **b.** "Hey Jealousy"/Gin Blossoms
27. **a.** "Kiss"/Prince
28. **b.** "Spoonman"/Soundgarden
29. **c.** "Don't You (Forget About Me)"/Simple Minds
30. **b.** "Epic"/Faith No More
31. **b.** "More Than Words Can Say"/Alias
32. **c.** "Are You Gonna Go My Way"/Lenny Kravitz
33. **b.** "Why Can't I Be You"/Cure
34. **a.** "Amazing"/Aerosmith
35. **c.** "Love is Strong"/Rolling Stones
36. **a.** "Say Something"/James
37. **a.** "Need You Tonight"/INXS
38. **a.** "Never a Time"/Phil Collins
39. **c.** "Disarm"/Smashing Pumpkins
40. **a.** "You Let Your Heart Go Too Fast"/Spin Doctors
41. **c.** "Big Time"/Peter Gabriel
42. **b.** "Free Fallin'"/Tom Petty
43. **a.** "EvenFlow"/Pearl Jam
44. **b.** "One Thing Lead to Another"/Fixx

45. b. "Rock and Roll Dreams Come Through"/Meat Loaf
46. b. "Welcome to the Jungle"/Guns 'N Roses
47. c. "Love Bites"/Def Leppard
48. a. "I'd Die for You"/Bon Jovi
49. a. "Too Much Information"/Duran Duran
50. c. "Raspberry Beret"/Prince